contents

Each example in this book is numbered. A specific CD track may contain more than one example. For instance Ex. 1 and Ex. 2 are both played on CD track 1.

introduction

ARPEGGIO CONNECTIONS is a unique collection of 164 cyclically repeating arpeggio studies, designed to provide the guitarist with a logical and effective method for developing fast, fluid arpeggio runs that move freely across the entire fretboard while outlining specific chordal harmonies. The two-fold concept is simple:

Section 1) to develop the ability to play fast and powerful arpeggios **ACROSS THE NECK** using hammer-ons and pull-offs for fluidity (non-shifting motion where the fretting hand stays in one area of the fretboard); and

Section 2) to develop the ability to play smooth and fast arpeggio runs while the fretting hand shifts **ALONG THE NECK** using slides (which I like to call "horizontal" motion, since the hand is moving sideways, parallel to the earth's horizon)

By developing complete non-shifting arpeggio control, and also developing complete position-shifting arpeggio control, the resulting effect is **whole neck fluid motion** that freely weaves together an established matrix system of arpeggio patterns and pathways. The design of the material in this book is highly scientific, having been developed through many years of shaping and crafting this concept. What you are holding in your hands is a manual for developing smooth, flowing arpeggio movement on the guitar, which is useful to ALL GUITARISTS in pursuit of virtuosity in ANY STYLE of music.

The student should feel free to go directly to the studies anywhere in the book, but is encouraged to *eventually* read and understand the ideas discussed in the appendix. The goal is to play blistering, continuous streams of fluid melodic lines that outline specific chords. The appendix addresses certain issues that are fundamental to this type of virtuosic control (such as how the organization of strict alternate picking is affected by hammers, pull-offs and slides). By playing the patterns and exercises herein on a regular basis for weeks, months, and years, the player's control over the instrument will continue to unfold and to grow ever more formidable and fierce.

This book is the first book in the **'FLUID SOLOING SERIES'**, a unified set of books that explain different aspects of whole neck fluid motion on the guitar. The soloing etudes marked "Comprehensive" are included to demonstrate some of the techniques from the other three books, as well as the techniques presented in this one, all used in combination to create an exciting soloing style that is flowing and varied in its melodic patterns. If you like the content of this book, check out the other books in the series as well. Good luck!

MEL BAY PRESENTS

FLUID SOLOING

BY TIM QUINN

MEL BAY GUITAR UNIVERSITY • MEL BAY GUITAR UNIVERSITY •

MBGU

BOOK 1 ARPEGGIOS FOR LEAD ROCK GUITAR

CD contents

1 Ex. 1-2	26 Ex. 39-40	51 Ex. 80-82	76 Ex. 119-121
2 Ex. 3-4	27 Ex. 41-42	52 Ex. 83-85	77 Ex. 122-124
3 Ex. 5-6	28 Ex. 43-44	53 Ex. 86	78 Ex. 125-127
4 Ex. 7-8	29 Ex. 45-46	54 Ex. 87-88	79 Ex. 128-130
5 Ex. 9-10	30 Ex. 47-48	55 Ex. 89-90	80 Ex. 131-133
6 Ex. 11-12	31 Ex. 49-50	56 Ex. 91	81 Ex. 134-136
7 Ex. 13-14	32 Ex. 51	57 Ex. 92	82 Ex. 137-139
8 Ex. 15-16	33 Ex. 52	58 Ex. 93	83 Ex. 140-142
9 Ex. 17	34 Ex. 53-54	59 Ex. 94	84 Ex. 143-145
10 Ex. 18	35 Ex. 55-56	60 Ex. 95	85 Ex. 146-148
11 Ex. 19	36 Ex. 57-58	61 Ex. 96	86 Ex. 149-151
12 Ex. 20	37 Ex. 59-60	62 Ex. 97	87 Ex. 152-154
13 Ex. 21	38 Ex. 61-62	63 Ex. 98	88 Ex. 155
14 Ex. 22	39 Ex. 63-64	64 Ex. 99	89 Ex. 156
15 Ex. 23-24	40 Ex. 65-66	65 Ex. 100	90 Ex. 157
16 Ex. 25-26	41 Ex. 67-68	66 Ex. 101	91 Ex. 158
17 Ex. 27-28	42 Ex. 69	67 Ex. 102	92 Ex. 159
18 Ex. 29	43 Ex. 70	68 Ex. 103	93 Ex. 160
19 Ex. 30	44 Ex. 71	69 Ex. 104	94 Ex. 161
20 Ex. 31	45 Ex. 72	70 Ex. 105	95 Ex. 162
21 Ex. 32	46 Ex. 73	71 Ex. 106	96 Ex. 163
22 Ex. 33	47 Ex. 74	72 Ex. 107-109	97 Ex. 164
23 Ex. 34	48 Ex. 75	73 Ex. 110-112	
24 Ex. 35-36	49 Ex. 76	74 Ex. 113-115	
25 Ex. 37-38	50 Ex. 77-79	75 Ex. 116-118	

MEL BAY ®

2 3 4 5 6 7 8 9 0

© 2009 BY MEL BAY PUBLICATIONS, INC., PACIFIC, MO 63069.
ALL RIGHTS RESERVED. INTERNATIONAL COPYRIGHT SECURED. B.M.I. MADE AND PRINTED IN U.S.A.
No part of this publication may be reproduced in whole or in part, or stored in a retrieval system, or transmitted in any form
or by any means, electronic, mechanical, photocopy, recording, or otherwise, without written permission of the publisher.

Visit us on the Web at www.melbay.com — E-mail us at email@melbay.com

acknowledgements

A heartfelt thanks goes out to all the teachers who profoundly impacted my own playing and learning…thank you Jack Petersen, Dan Haerle, Rich Matteson, and Tom Johnson at the University of North Texas, as well as to my teachers at Berklee College of Music. To the musicians who have been so inspiring…Steve Morse, Pat Martino, John Coltrane, Eric Johnson, Chick Corea, Jimi Hendrix, Frank Zappa, Barney Kessell, Wes Montgomery, Stevie Ray Vaughan, Albert King, Jeff Beck, Steve Vai, Dexter Gordon, Cannonball Adderly, Joe Satriani, Igor Stravinsky, Eddie Van Halen, Al DiMeola, Greg Howe, Joe Pass, Robben Ford, Vinnie Moore, Allan Holdsworth, and Carlos Santana; for the teachings of Paramahansa Yogananda; to Bill Bay and the fine staff at Mel Bay Publications, Inc.; to Bruce Saunders for his caring engraving; to Dave Austin and George Sanchez for their generous assistance; to Josquin DePres at Track Star Studios for much inspiration and guidance; to the many students who have been indispensable in helping me streamline these materials; to my parents who provided the music education and encouraged the young performer; and especially to my wife, Mari, who lovingly tolerated the thousands of hours with me at the guitar while I formulated these concepts…thank you.

The title of this book is "Fluid Soloing: Arpeggios for Lead Rock Guitar". Its purpose is to teach you how to solo over chord changes using strictly arpeggios only, as opposed to using scales. Section I of this book presents a special collection of non-shifting arpeggios for the guitarist, designed for developing blistering speed and maximum range while keeping the fretting hand in one location on the neck. These are the fundamental arpeggio components, necessary to facilitate the eventual connection of arpeggios. So, please understand that the activities of connecting arpeggios really begin on page 37. Go right there and beyond for arpeggio connections at any time you wish. Do understand, though, that most of Section I of this book is in itself a practical manual of arpeggio non-shifting fingerings for every guitarist. In order to develop the connection of arpeggios, we must start with these basic non-shifting shapes. It is all about understanding the anatomy of the guitar fretboard and its inherent arpeggio shapes. You will be instructed in how to connect them in activities beginning on page 37 and beyond. But you needn't learn all the shapes in Section I before moving on to Section 2. Just begin by practicing a few of the shapes between pages 8-36. But then jump ahead, too! For instance, try pages 38, 49, 67, 84, 88 or 90 for some challenging fun, while you continue to pursue the material between pages 8-36. There is enough material in this book to keep you busy for the next two years or more. This is truly a wizard's handbook to arpeggio usage. Have fun!

Tim Quinn

a few important points about this book

1. Most of the examples in this book are repetitive exercises. After you've learned them as written, try starting the melodic patterns from a different location. For example, if a pattern begins with an ascending motion, and then goes into a descending motion (so that it can start over), try starting the pattern at the point at which it begins to descend instead. This greatly increases the usefulness of the pattern.

2. When working on a given pattern, memorize it so you can direct all of your visual and mental attention toward your hands and the guitar. Reading the exercise off the paper requires one third of your attention. Better to play a pattern from memory with eyes on the hands, thereby putting your mental energy into the execution of the passage, rather than into reading it.

3. Memorize these patterns, and then play them regularly for a period of months. While this is a long-term investment, it will result in your ability to outline any chord with a blazing arpeggio run, no matter where you are on the neck. Persistent, regular practice will make these patterns easy to play.

4. Cultivate the ability to play musical passages as a result of imagining the sound. After memorizing a pattern, sing the melodies internally as you **let your hands play the notes**. Let go of intellectual control. Get used to playing music purely as a result of channeling the sound you hear in your head, as opposed to it being an exercise in physical execution. After all, this IS music. The best musicians are those who manage to incorporate their musical imagination and feeling into their striving for willful technical control. This is wherein lies the magic of great improvisation. Feel it.

5. Occasionally you will encounter an indication to hammer the very first note on a given string with the left hand, as opposed to picking it. I call this a "HAMMER-ON FROM NOWHERE." This is done as a way to increase fluidity and speed, but if you want to, you can go ahead and pick it.

6. Another technique needing clarification is the "TRANSFER." The transfer involves two notes on the same string, where only the first note is picked. Sound the second note by hammering to an arbitrary note on the same string (one or two frets above the first note) as the hand simultaneously and abruptly slides into the targeted higher note. See the tablature symbols key.

7. Be sure to read the appendix at the end of the book, entitled *GUIDELINES FOR USING THIS BOOK.* Here you will find much useful insight, including a detailed description of strict alternate picking and its application.

8. Occasionally try light palm muting near the bridge (as you pick) for a tighter and faster sound and feel.

9. All examples in this book sound great with either a clean or distorted tone.

10. When encountering two consecutive notes on adjacent strings that are played with the same finger (as in Ex. No. 3), roll the fingertip from one note to the next, rather than lifting it.

section one ▸ rapid-fire arpeggios

important points for study

▸ This section presents a special collection of **non-shifting** arpeggios for the guitarist, designed for blistering speed and maximum range while keeping the fretting hand in one location on the neck.

▸ <u>Each arpeggio is presented in two rhythmic configurations</u>; one for 16th note motion, and one for triplet motion. Play each arpeggio continuously and repetitively, striving for absolute familiarity and ease of execution.

▸ Arpeggios are presented here for: **Minor 7, Dominant 7, Major 7, Diminished 7, Min. 7(♭5), Min. 6, Major Triadic,** and **Minor Triadic** applications.

▸ Left-hand fingerings are extremely important, so observe the indicated fingerings. Arpeggios that span an area of 6-7 frets (No. 3, for example) require a left-hand neck position where the thumb is low on the neck, with the fingers in a more parallel line with the frets, with the hand reaching up to the neck from below.

▸ In order to play these patterns fast, the order of pickstrokes may need to be studied. **Strict alternate picking** (as explained in the appendix) means that each note is assigned a down or an upstroke from the start. A slide, hammer, or pull-off simply replaces a pickstroke, but does not change the predetermined picking assignment. A complete understanding of this is essential (see appendix for a full discussion of strict alternate picking). Without proper application of strict alternate picking, most guitarists will struggle with these repetitive patterns when they are played fast. Strict alternate picking eliminates the struggle, so…learn it! Later, after establishing picking control, try palm muting with the right hand as you pick.

▸ To increase the usability of these patterns, also learn to play each arpeggio starting from its highest note, beginning with a descending direction.

▸ Practical application of these arpeggios is demonstrated in several soloing etudes at the end of this chapter.

▸ Each set of arpeggios is referred to with two numbers, indicating the string on which the root note is located, and the finger that plays it. For example, all the arpeggios in SET 5-1 have their lowest root on the 5th string, fretted with the 1st finger.

outline for this chapter

I. Non-Shifting Arpeggios, in SEVEN SETS

II. Practice Suggestions and Soloing Etudes

rapid-fire arpeggio patterns (set 5-1)

Arpeggios with the root on the 5th string, fretted with the 1st finger.

All arpeggios in this set are shown with "E" as the root. Each arpeggio is shown both in 16th notes and in triplets. In the initial stages of memorization, the student may wish to focus only on the first measure of each two bar pattern.

Play each arpeggio repetitively to establish muscle memory.

 ▸ **No. 1** (Ex. 1-2)

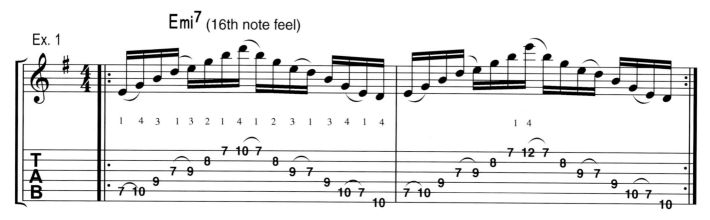

 ▸ **No. 2** (Ex. 3-4)

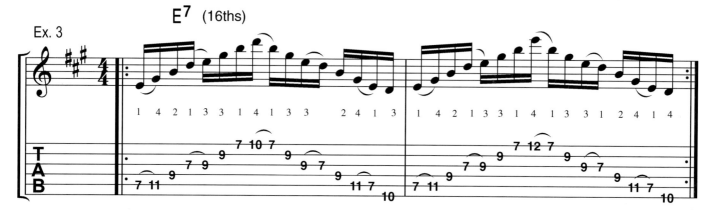

Ex. 4

E^7 (triplets)

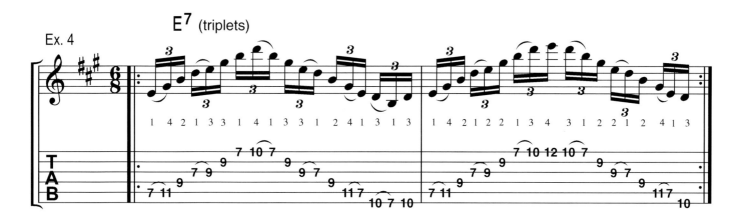

With so many patterns to memorize, a managed approach to learning is helpful initially. Focus on being able to play the 16th note version of _only the Maj.7, Dom.7, mi7, and dim.7_ arpeggios, played consecutively, on after the other. Do this in each arpeggio set. This will serve to establish familiarity with each set.

 ▸ **No. 3** (Ex. 5-6)

Ex. 5

E$_{MAJ}^7$ (16ths)

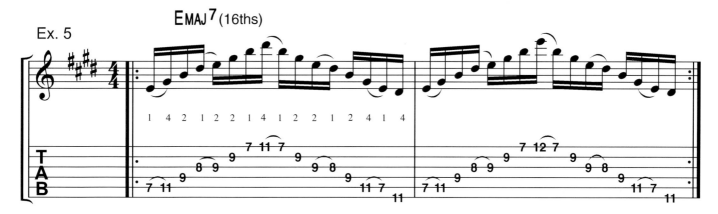

Ex. 6

E$_{MAJ}^7$ (triplets)

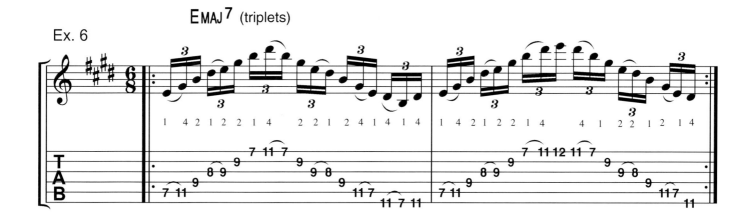

▶ **No. 4** (Ex. 7-8)

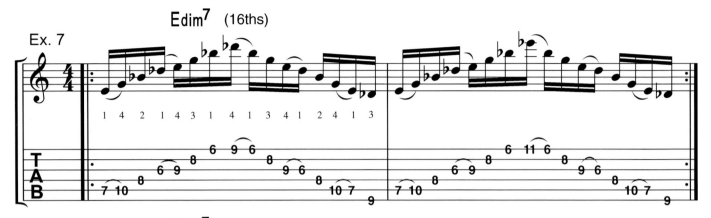

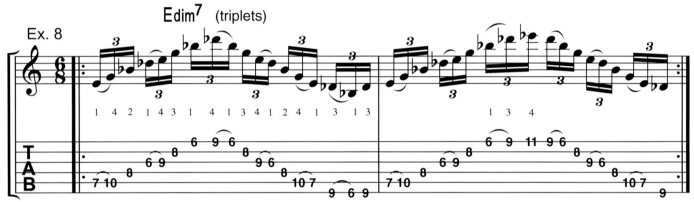

▶ **No. 5** (Ex. 9-10)

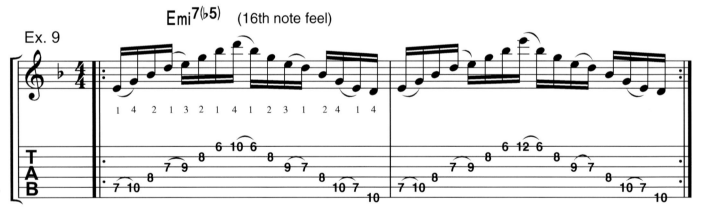

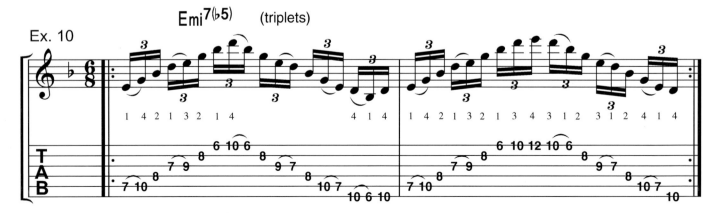

▸ No. 6 (Ex. 11-12)

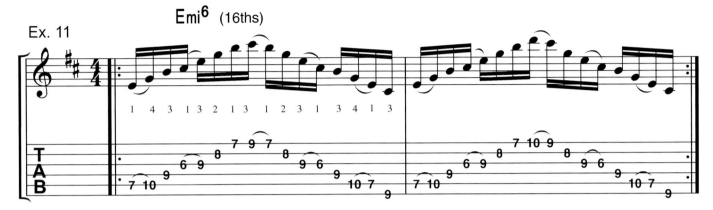

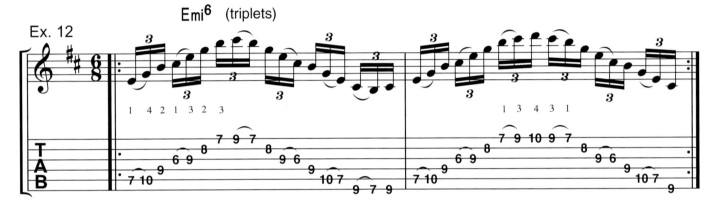

 ▸ No. 7 (Ex. 13-14)

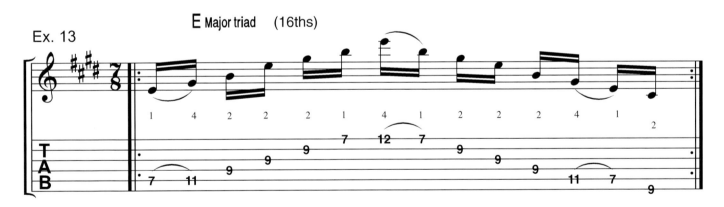

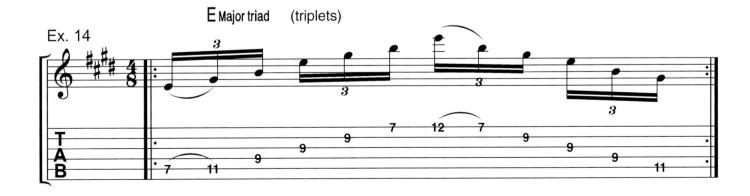

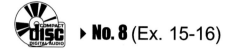 **No. 8** (Ex. 15-16)

Ex. 15

E minor triad   (16ths)

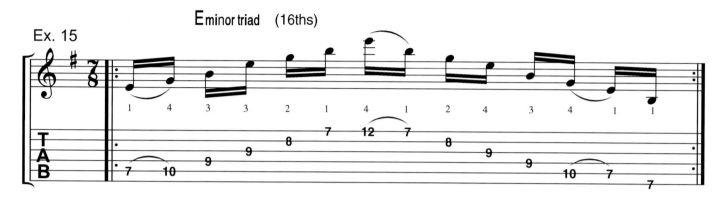

Ex. 16

E minor triad   (triplets)

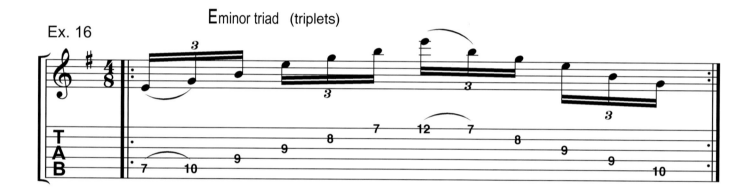

▸ **Don't forget...**It is highly recommended that you learn to pick each arpeggio with the strict alternate picking approach, as is described in the appendix of this book. Strict alternate picking is completely compatible with patterns that utilize hammers and pulls. Read the explanation in the appendix.

rapid-fire arpeggio patterns (set 6-1)

Arpeggios with the root on the 6th string, fretted with the 1st finger.

All arpeggios in this set are shown with "B" as the root. Practice all arpeggios in both 16ths and in triplets. In the initial stages of memorization, the student may wish to focus only on the first measure of each two bar pattern.

Play each arpeggio repetitively to establish muscle memory.

▸ **No. 9** (Ex. 17)

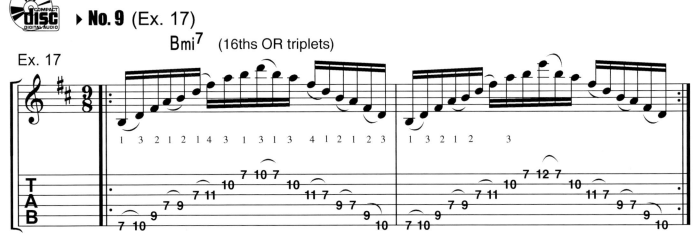

▸ **No. 10** (Ex. 18)

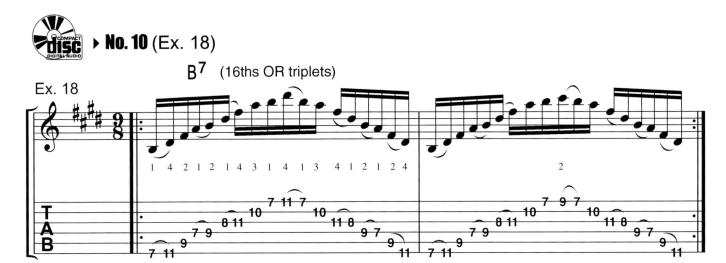

▸ **No. 11** (Ex. 19)

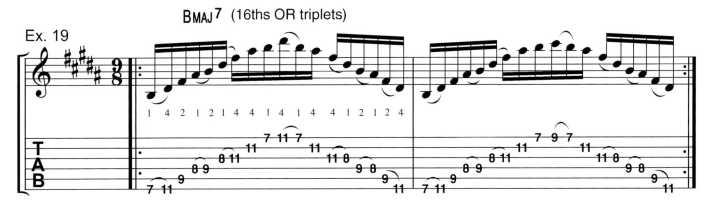

No. 12 (Ex. 20)

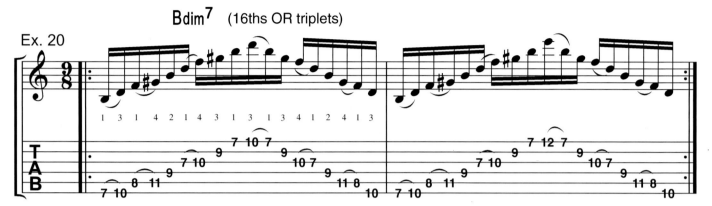

No. 13 (Ex. 21)

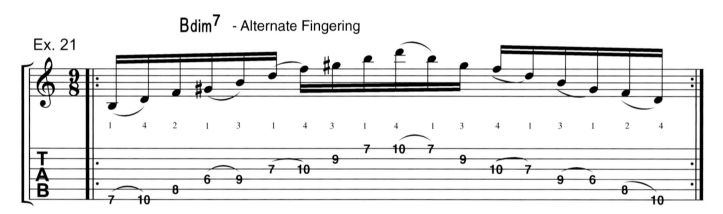

No. 14 (Ex. 22)

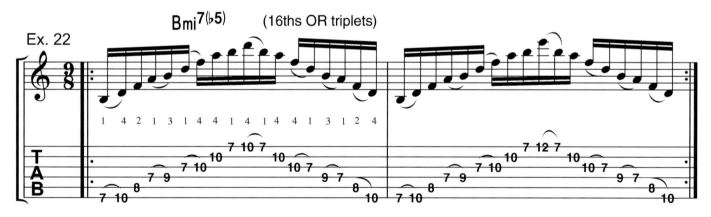

The **"hammer-on-from-nowhere"** is best executed when the fretting fingers are kept parallel to the frets, with the thumb low on the back of the neck. Swing the pinky-side of the hand with centrifugal force as you execute this hammer-on. (Remember: This technique is optional...you may simply pick the note instead.)

▶ No. 15 (Ex. 23-24)

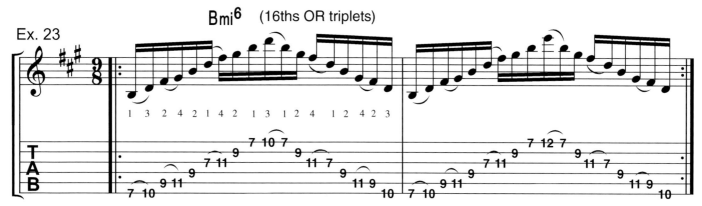

Bmi⁶ (16ths OR triplets)

Ex. 23

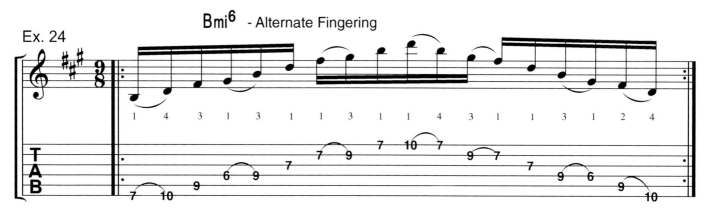

Bmi⁶ - Alternate Fingering

Ex. 24

▶ No. 16 (Ex. 25-26)

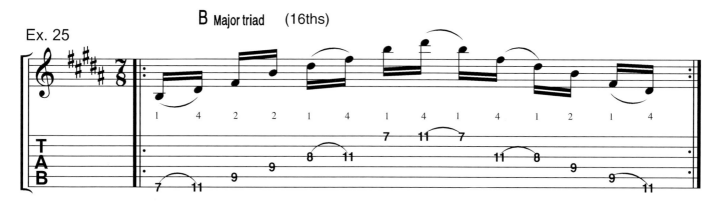

B Major triad (16ths)

Ex. 25

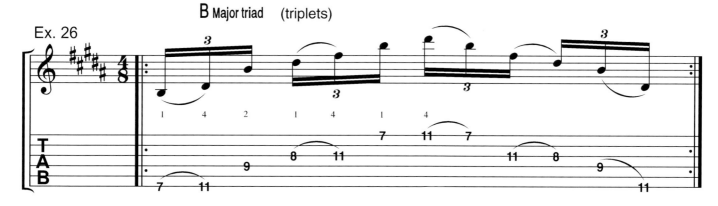

B Major triad (triplets)

Ex. 26

▶ **No. 17** (Ex. 27-28)

With so many patterns to memorize, try starting with just four arpeggios from each set...the 16th note feel Maj.7, Dom.7, mi.7 and dim.7. These arpeggios sound great when play consecutively in this order, and will serve as a foundational reference when it comes time to learn the other arpeggios in a given set.

rapid-fire arpeggio patterns (set 5-4)

Arpeggios with the root on the 5th string, fretted with the 1st finger.

All arpeggios in this set are shown with "A" as the root. Practice all arpeggios in both 16ths and in triplets. Most of the arpeggios in this set are presented with the root as the second note, which increases their fluidity.

Play each arpeggio repetitively to establish muscle memory.

* When playing Exercises 29-34 with a triplet feel, change the articulation of the last 3 notes to pick/pull-off/pick.

▶ **No. 18** (Ex. 29)

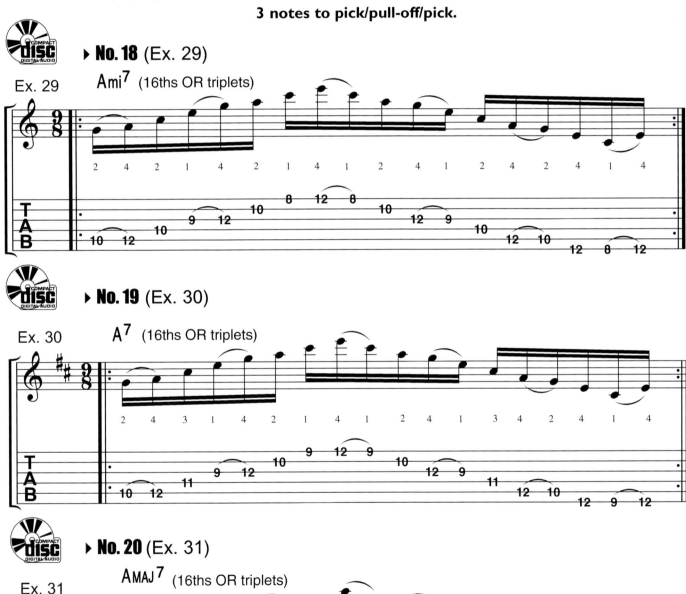

▶ **No. 19** (Ex. 30)

▶ **No. 20** (Ex. 31)

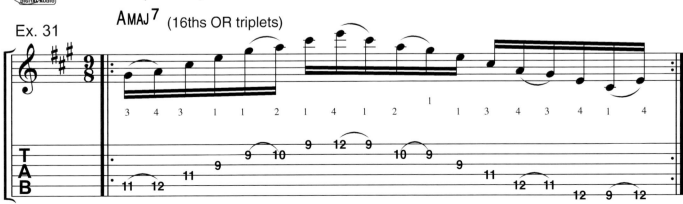

No. 21 (Ex. 32)

Adim⁷ (16ths OR triplets)

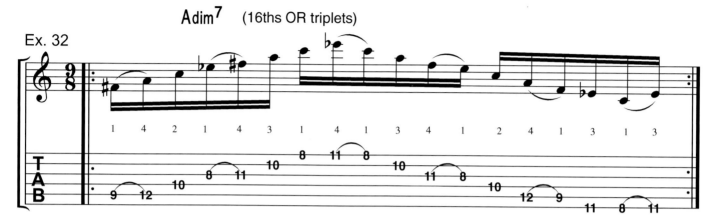

No. 22 (Ex. 33)

Ami⁷⁽♭⁵⁾ (16ths OR triplets)

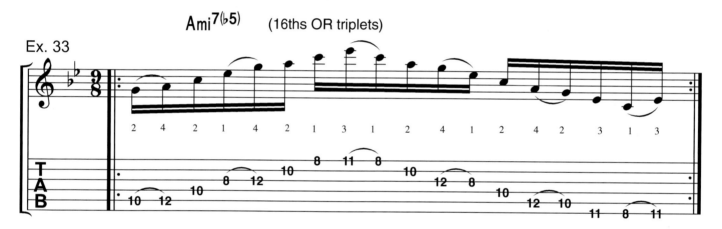

No. 23 (Ex. 34)

Ami⁶ (16ths OR triplets)

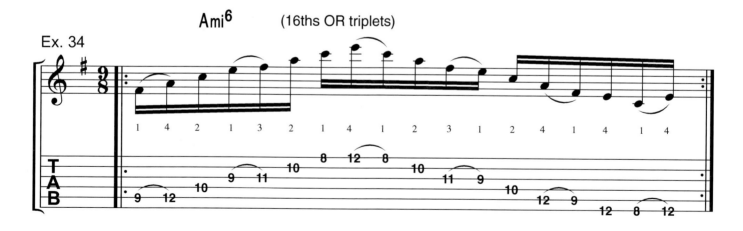

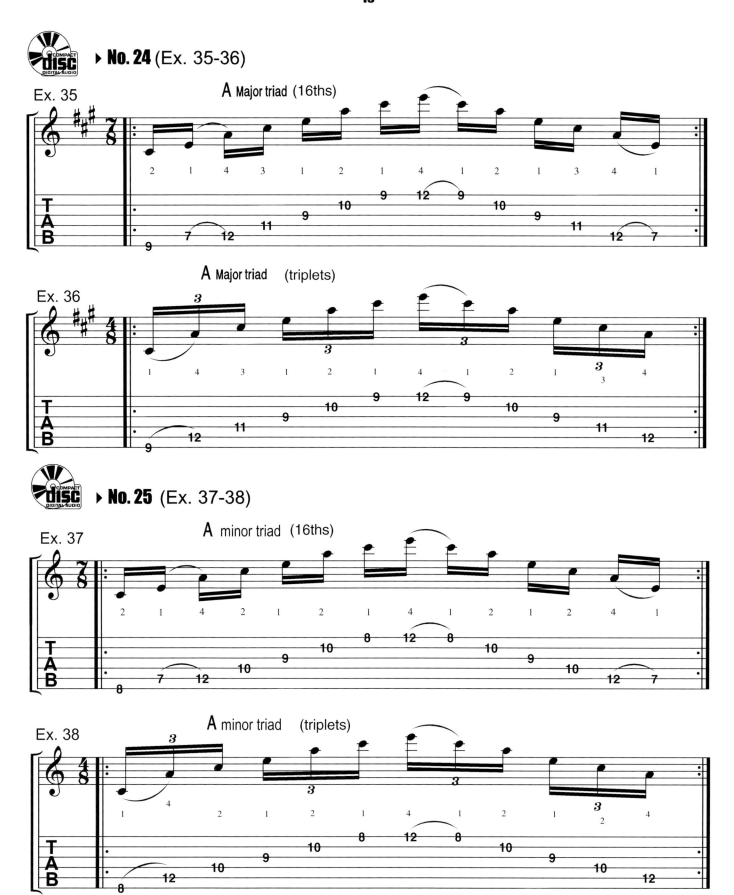

When attempting challenging patterns in alternate picking, it may be helpful to try light palm-muting near the bridge, especially on arpeggios that are primarily one-note-per-string (as in the above arpeggio). Also, watch the pick move across the strings as you go through the arpeggio. This will help you settle into efficient use of motion.

rapid-fire arpeggio patterns (set 6-4)

Arpeggios with the root on the 6th string, fretted with the 4th finger.

All arpeggios in this set are shown with "D" as the root. Each arpeggio is shown in both 16ths and in triplets. Most of the arpeggios in this set are presented with the root as the second note, which increases their fluidity.

Play each arpeggio repetitively to establish muscle memory.

In this set of arpeggios, the Dom.7, Maj.7 and Major Triadic arpeggios actually use the 3rd finger to fret the root of the arpeggio.

▸ **No. 26** (Ex. 39-40)

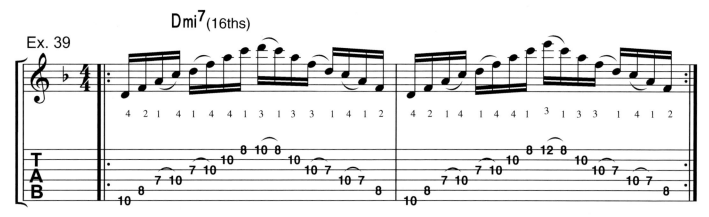

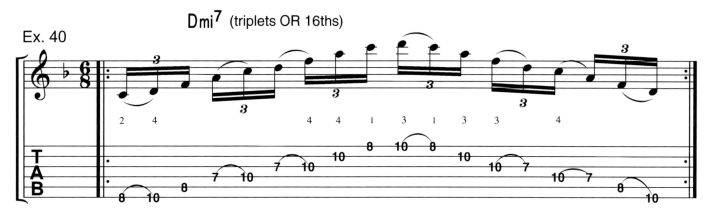

▶ **No. 27** (Ex. 41-42)

Ex. 41

D^7 (16ths)

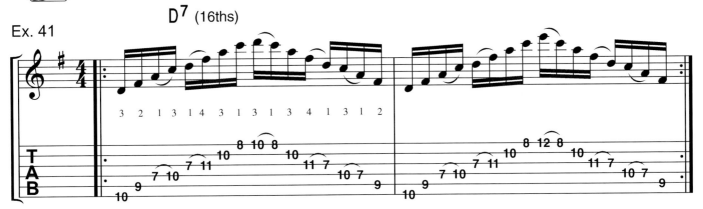

Ex. 42 D^7 (triplets)

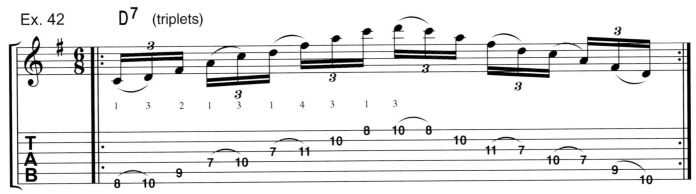

▶ **No. 28** (Ex. 43-44)

Ex. 43

D MAJ^7 (16ths)

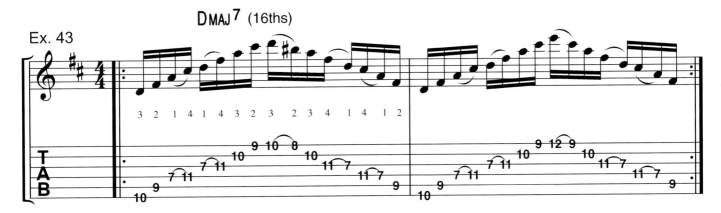

Ex. 44 D MAJ^7 (triplets OR 16ths)

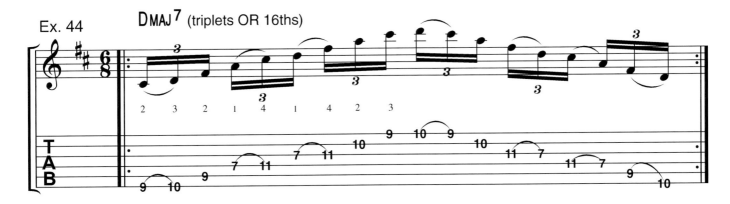

 **No. 29** (Ex. 45-46)

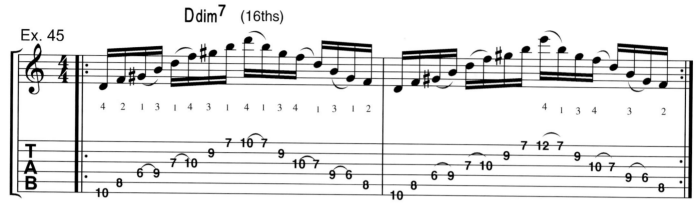

Ex. 45 — Ddim⁷ (16ths)

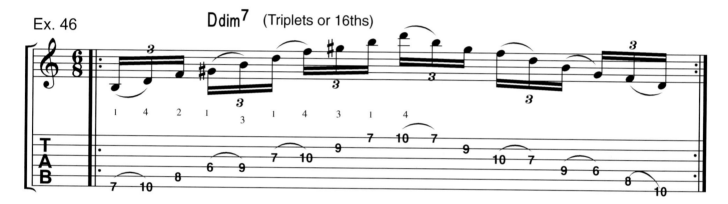

Ex. 46 — Ddim⁷ (Triplets or 16ths)

 **No. 30** (Ex. 47-48)

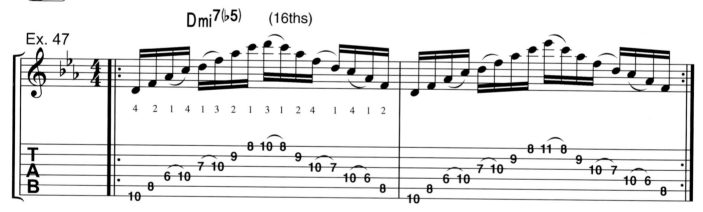

Ex. 47 — Dmi⁷(♭5) (16ths)

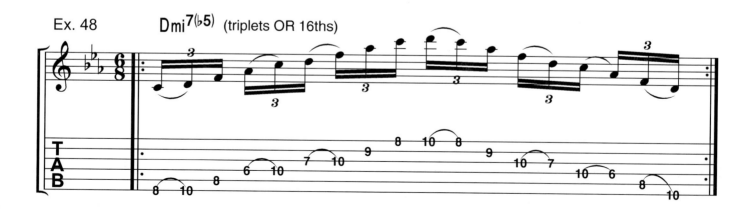

Ex. 48 — Dmi⁷(♭5) (triplets OR 16ths)

No. 31 (Ex. 49-50)

Ex. 49

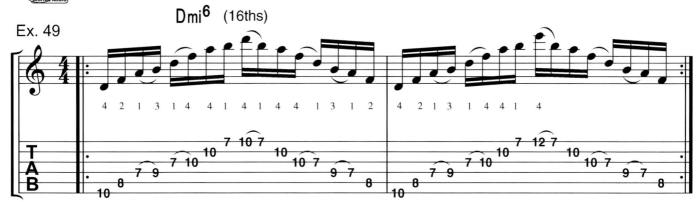

Ex. 50

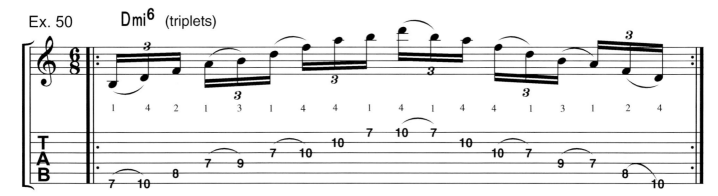

No. 32 (Ex. 51)

Ex. 51

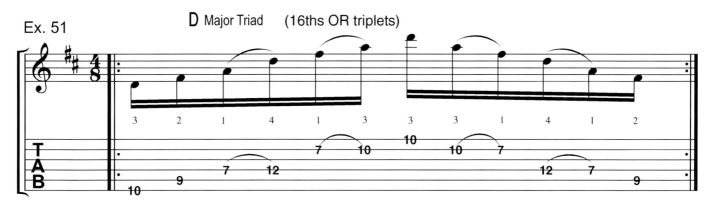

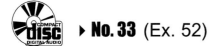

No. 33 (Ex. 52)

Ex. 52

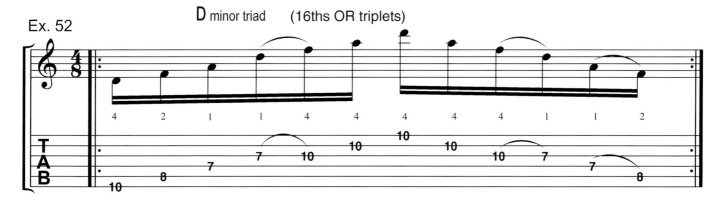

rapid-fire arpeggio patterns (set 4-1)

Arpeggios with the root on the 4th string, fretted with the 1st finger.

All arpeggios in this set are shown with "A" as the root. Each arpeggio is shown in both 16ths and in triplets. Most of the arpeggios in this set are presented with the root as the second note, which increases their fluidity.

Play each arpeggio repetitively to establish muscle memory.

▸ **No. 34** (Ex. 53-54)

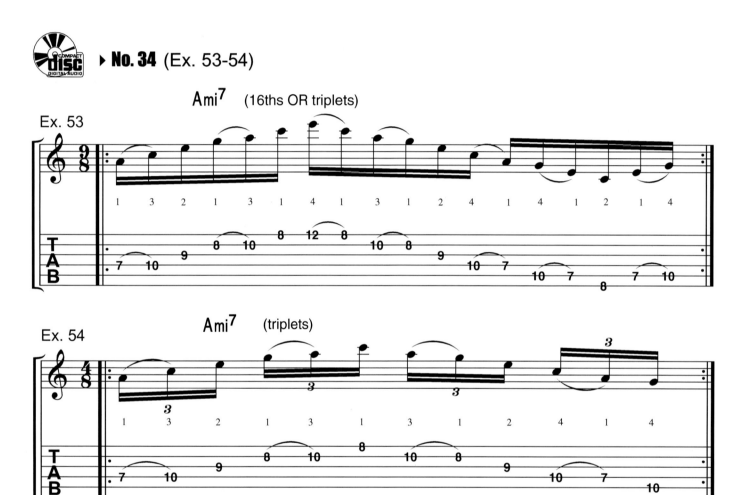

▸ **No. 35** (Ex. 55-56)

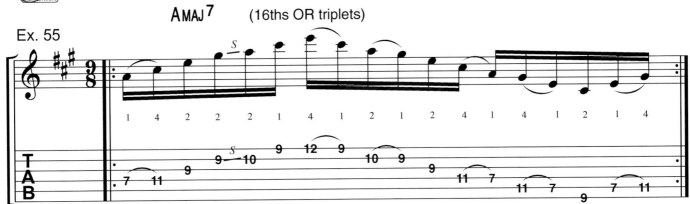

Ex. 55

A MAJ 7   (16ths OR triplets)

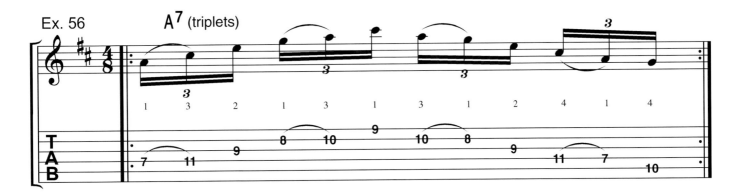

Ex. 56

A 7 (triplets)

▸ **No. 36** (Ex. 57-58)

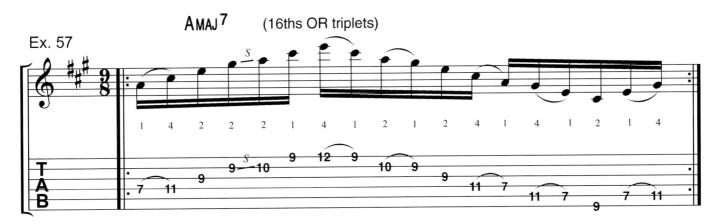

Ex. 57

A MAJ 7   (16ths OR triplets)

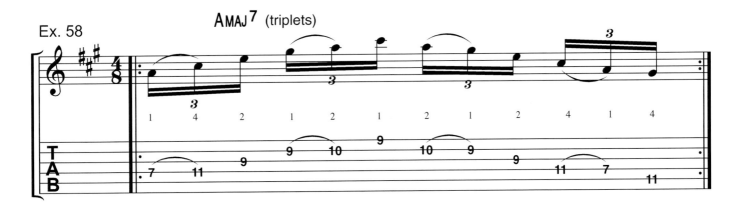

Ex. 58

A MAJ 7 (triplets)

No. 37 (Ex. 59-60)

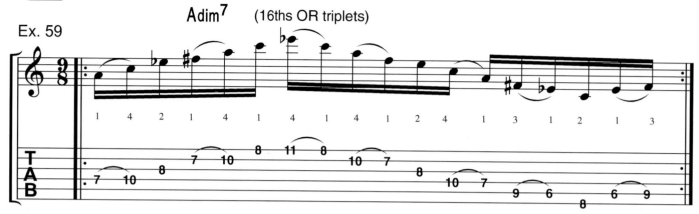

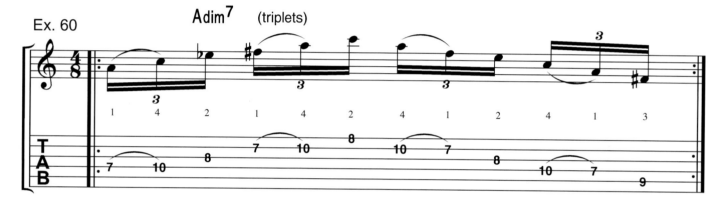

 No. 38 (Ex. 61-62)

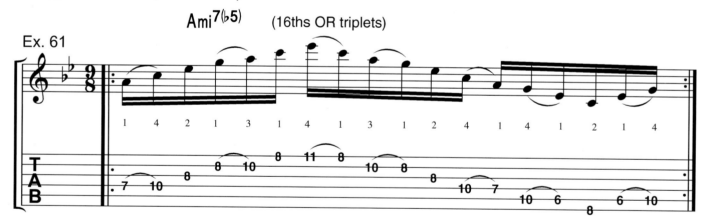

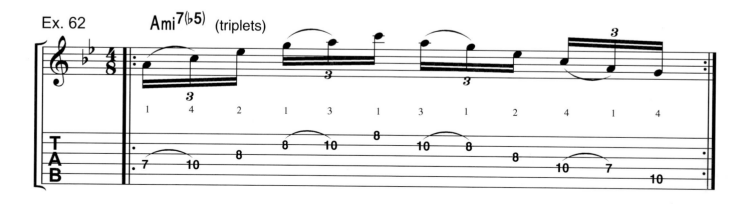

▶ **No. 39** (Ex. 63-64)

Ex. 63

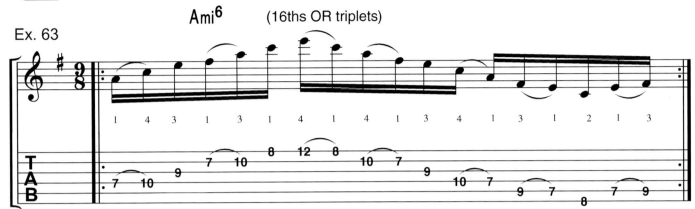

Ex. 64

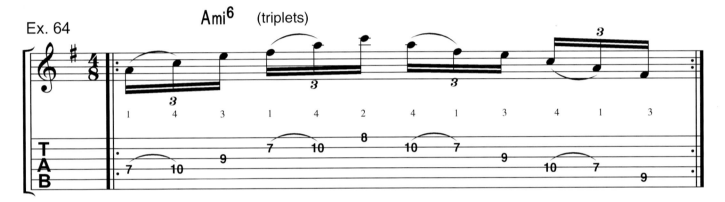

▶ **No. 40** (Ex. 65-66)

Ex. 65

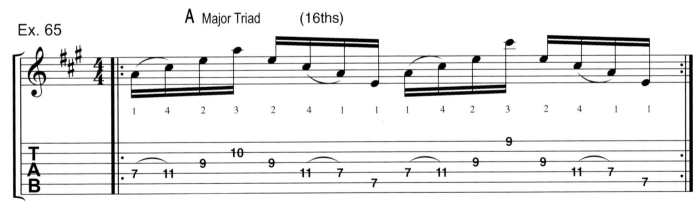

Ex. 66

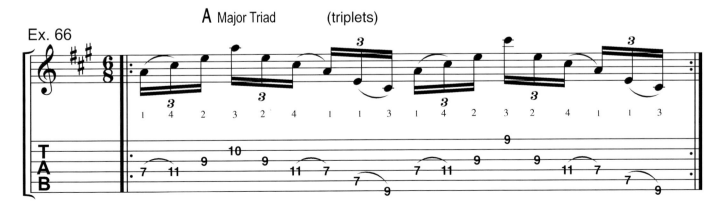

No. 41 (Ex. 67-68)

A Minor Triad   (16ths)

Ex. 67

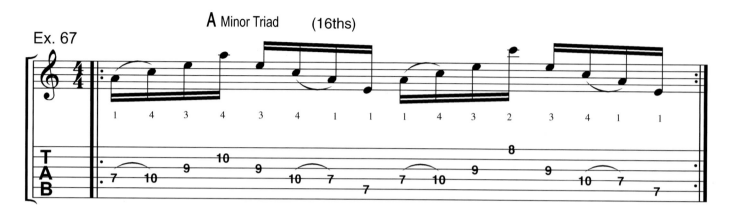

A minor triad   (triplets)

Ex. 68

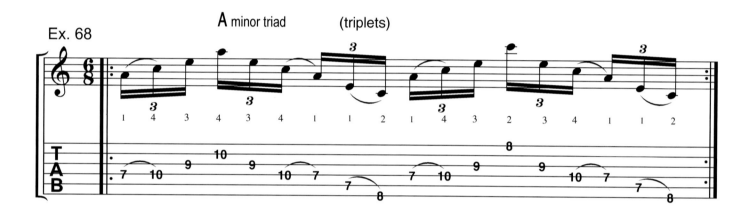

rapid-fire arpeggio patterns (set 6-2)

Arpeggios with the root on the 6th string, fretted with the 2nd finger.

All arpeggios in this set are shown with "D" as the root. Each arpeggio is shown in both 16ths and in triplets.

Play each arpeggio repetitively to establish muscle memory.

 ▸ **No. 42** (Ex. 69)

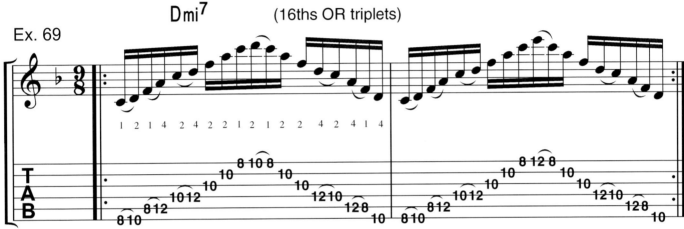

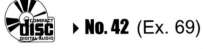 ▸ **No. 43** (Ex. 70)

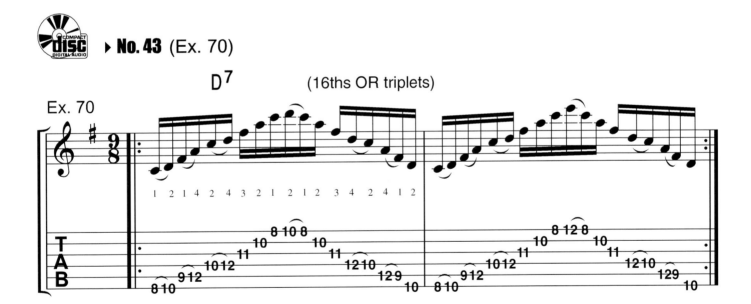

No. 44 (Ex. 71)

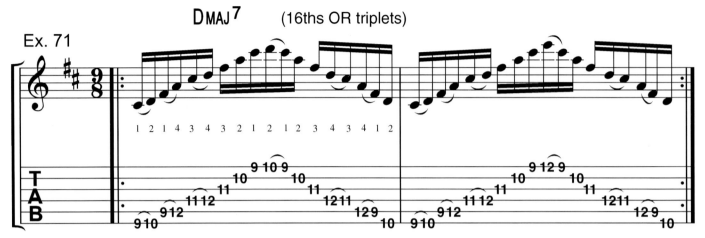

No. 45 (Ex. 72)

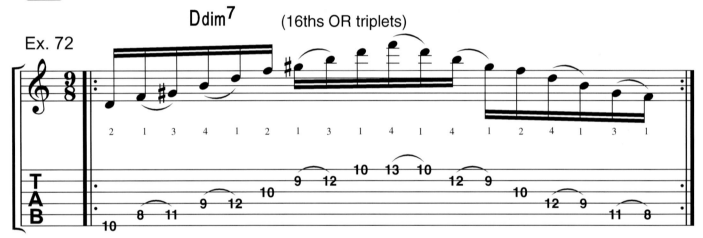

No. 46 (Ex. 73)

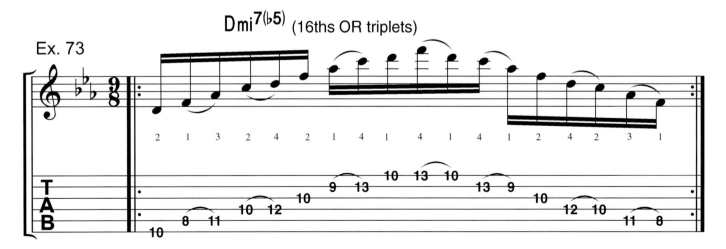

▶ **No. 47** (Ex. 74)

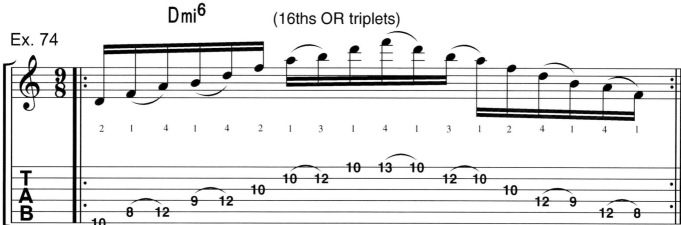

▶ **No. 48** (Ex. 75)

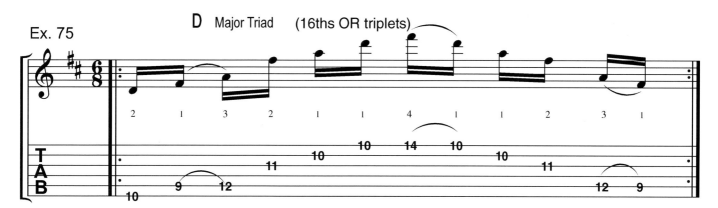

▶ **No. 49** (Ex. 76)

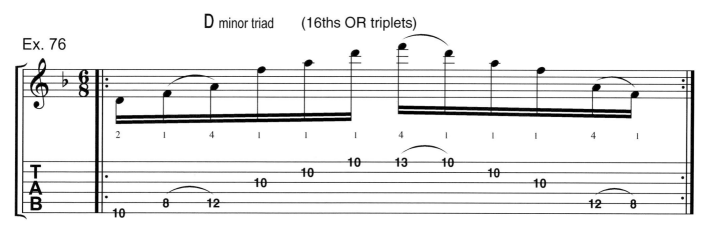

rapid-fire arpeggio patterns (set 5-2)

Arpeggios with the root on the 5th string, fretted with the 2nd finger.

All arpeggios in this set are shown with "G" as the root. Each arpeggio is shown in both 16ths and in triplets. (The min7(♭5) and min6 are shown with the 3rd finger on the root.)

Play each arpeggio repetitively to establish muscle memory.

 ▶ **No. 50** (Ex. 77-79)

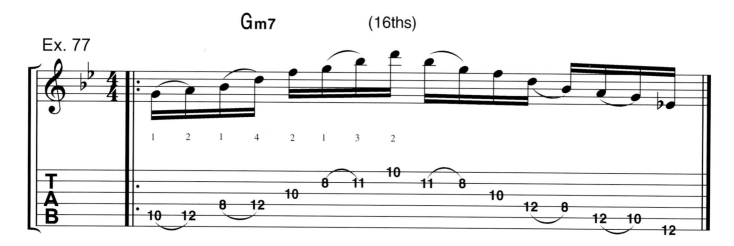

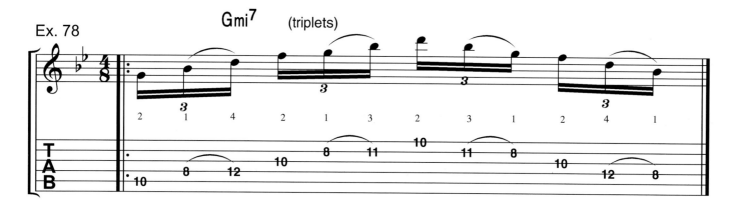

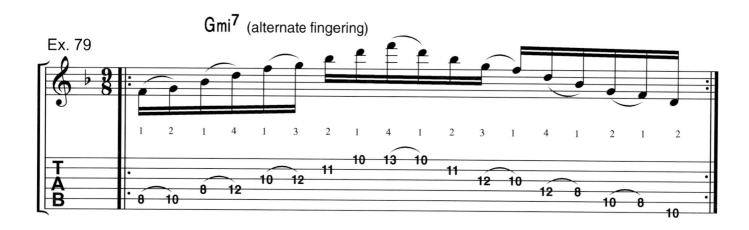

▸ **No. 51** (Ex. 80-82)

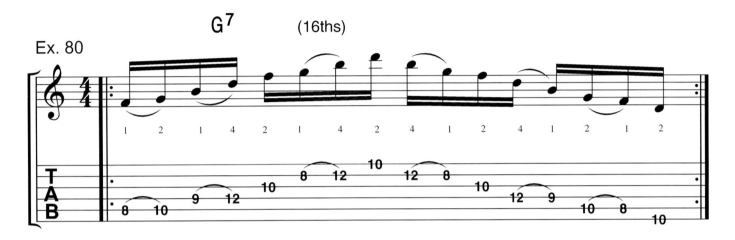

Ex. 80

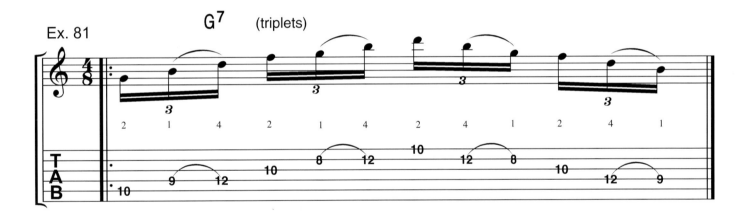

Ex. 81

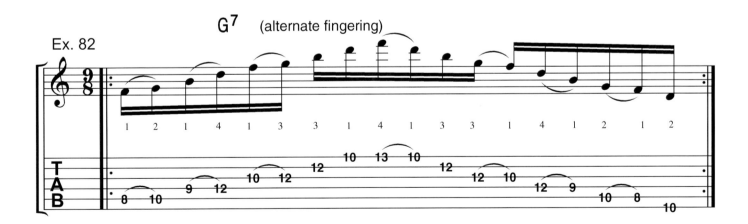

Ex. 82

▶ **No. 52** (Ex. 83-85)

GMAJ7 (16ths)

Ex. 83

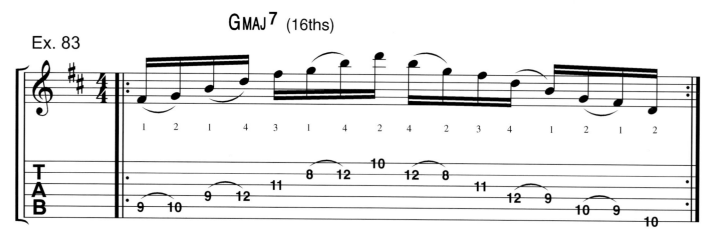

Ex. 84

GMAJ7 (triplets)

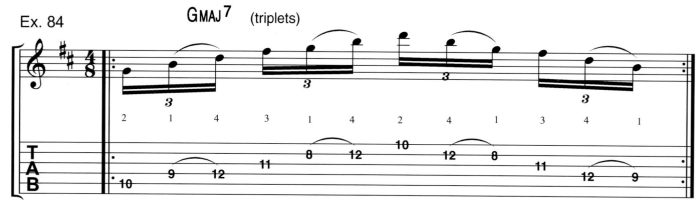

GMAJ7 (alternate fingering)

Ex. 85

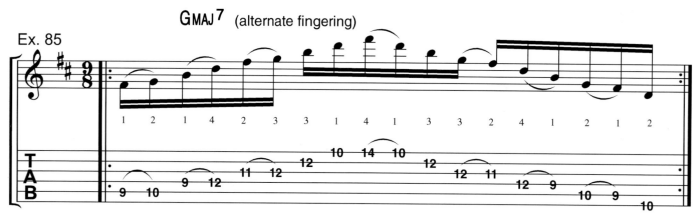

▶ **No. 53** (Ex. 86)

Gdim7 (16ths OR triplets)

Ex. 86

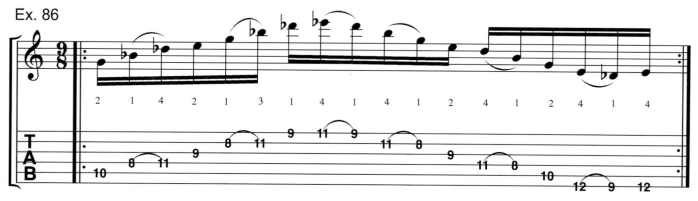

▶ **No. 54** (Ex. 87-88)

Ex. 87

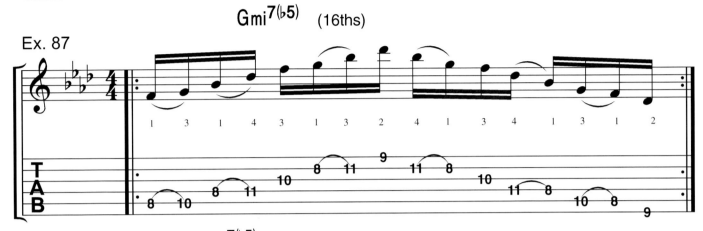

Ex. 88

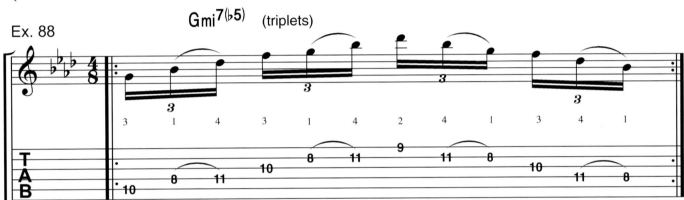

▶ **No. 55** (Ex. 89-90)

Ex. 89

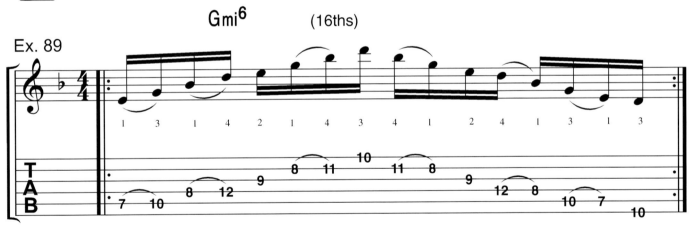

Ex. 90

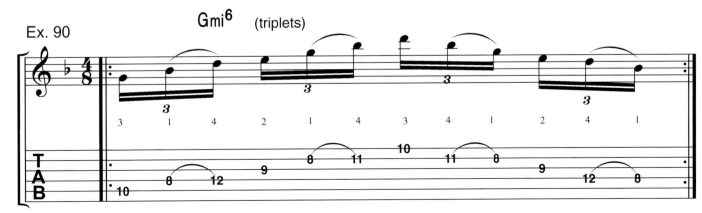

▸ **No. 56** (Ex. 91)

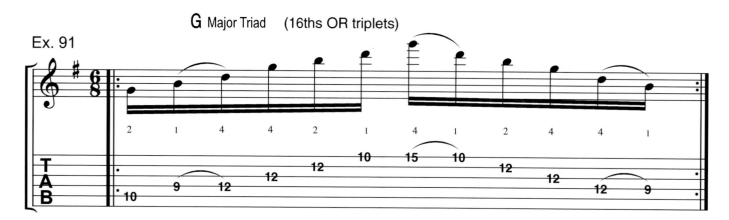

 ▸ **No. 57** (Ex. 92)

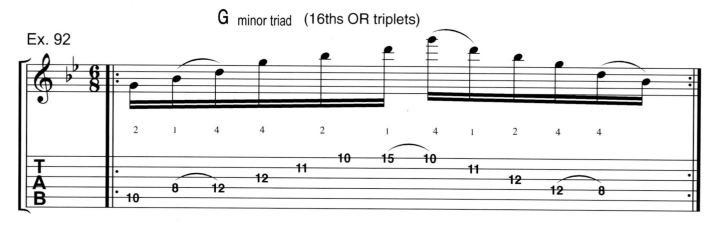

soloing etudes & practice suggestions

(using rapid-fire arpeggios)

practice suggestion #1

Playing all arpeggios (from a given set) consecutively to imprint into muscle memory.

In this demonstration, we are using SET 1-5, and the arpeggios are played with a 16th note feel. Exercise the same series of arpeggios in their triplet forms as well. Then, repeat this same procedure for EACH ARPEGGIO SET!.

Play each arpeggio twice, then move on to the next arpeggio. Practice daily

 ▸ **No. 58** (Ex. 93)

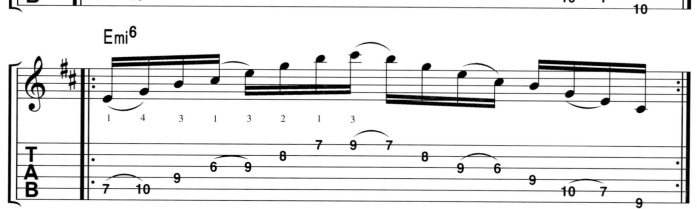

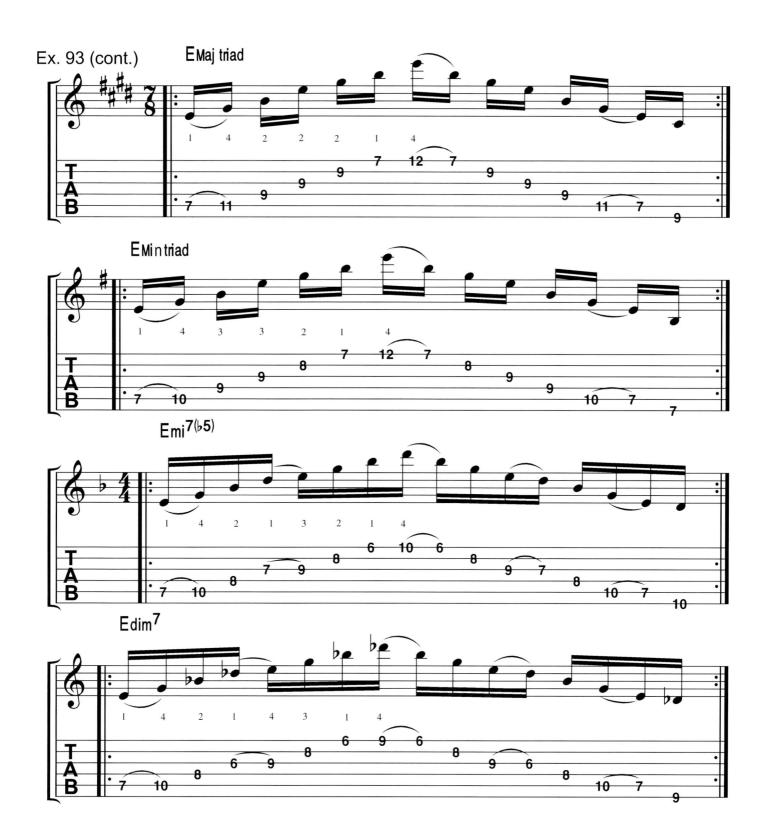

Ex. 93 (cont.)

practice suggestion #1a

Playing all arpeggios (from a given set) consecutively to imprint into muscle memory.

In this demonstration, we are using SET 6-1, and the arpeggios are played with a triplet feel. In addition, each arpeggio is started from its highest note. Practice EACH ARPEGGIO SET with this type of activity.

Play each arpeggio twice, then move on to the next arpeggio. Practice daily.

 ▸ **No. 59** (Ex. 94)

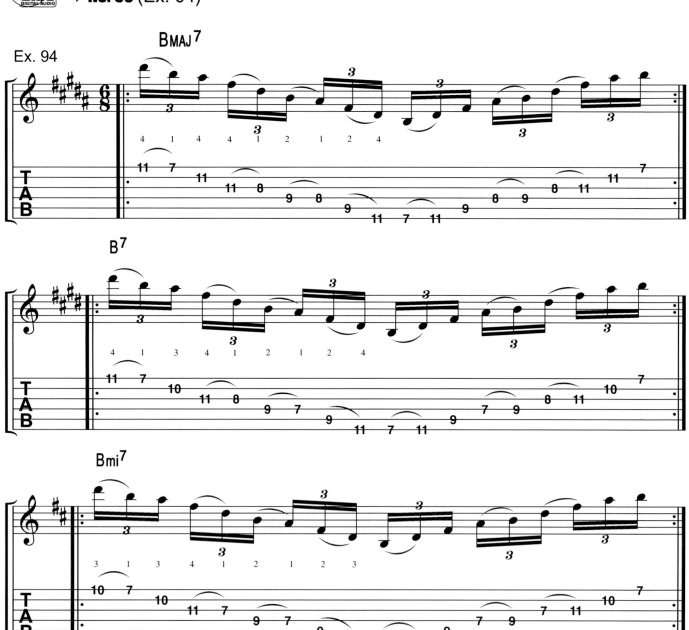

▸ No. 94 (cont.)

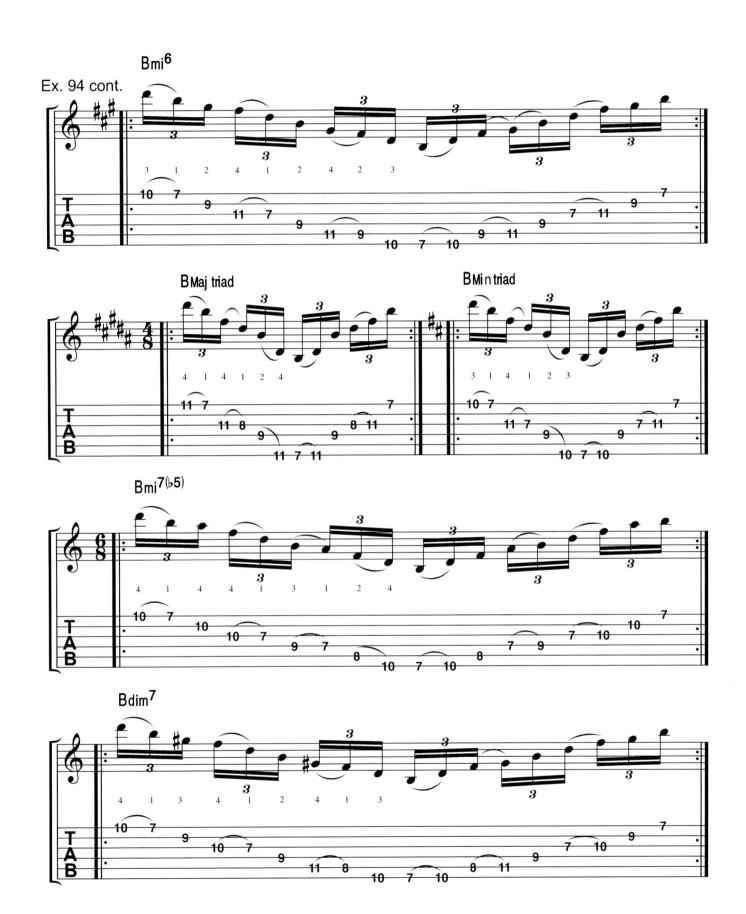

practice suggestion #2

Playing one arpeggio type through the cycle of 4ths, in one area of the neck.

In this study, the Maj7 arpeggio is played in all 12 keys, with the fretting hand positioned around the 7th fret. This is an effective way to imprint arpeggios into muscle memory and increase familiarity and availability.

Play each arpeggio twice, then move on to the next arpeggio. Practice daily.

 ▸ **No. 60** (Ex. 95)

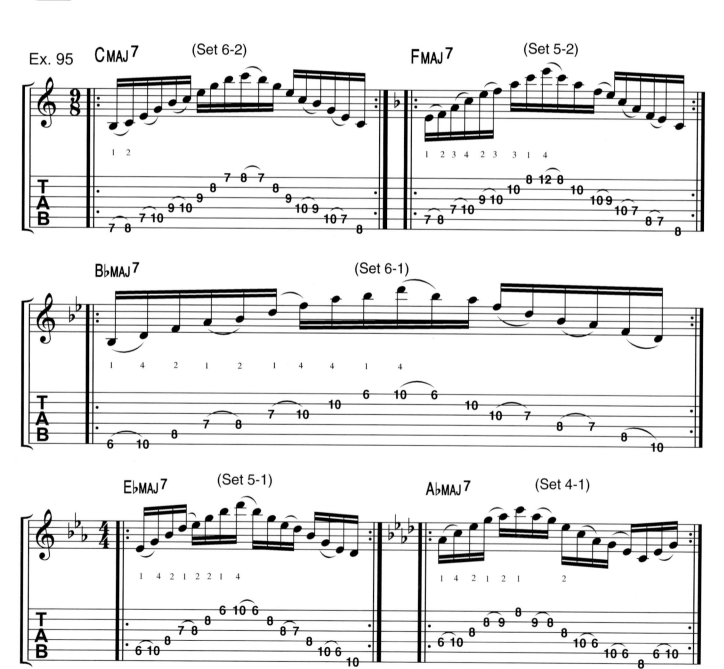

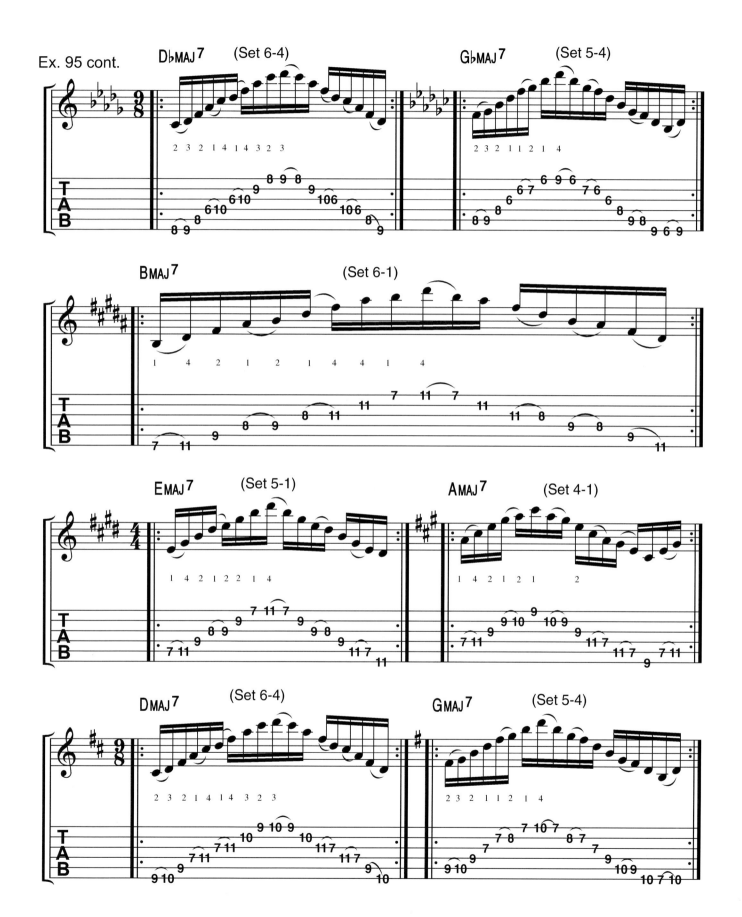

practice suggestion #2a

Playing one arpeggio type through the cycle of 4ths, in one area of the neck.

In this study, the dim7 arpeggio is played in all 12 keys, with the fretting hand positioned around the 9th fret, and a triplet feel is used. Practice suggestions #2 and #2a should be applied to all arpeggio types.

Play each arpeggio twice, then move on to the next arpeggio.

▶ **No. 61** (Ex. 96)

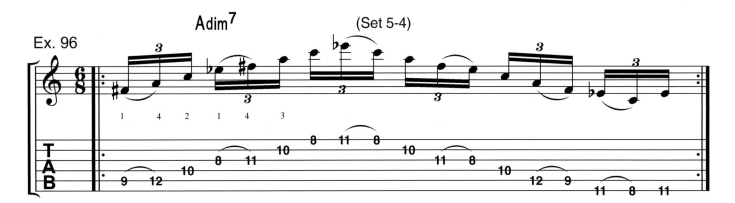

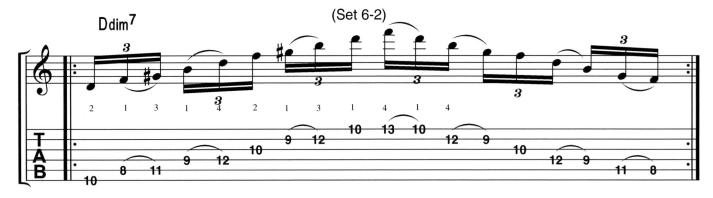

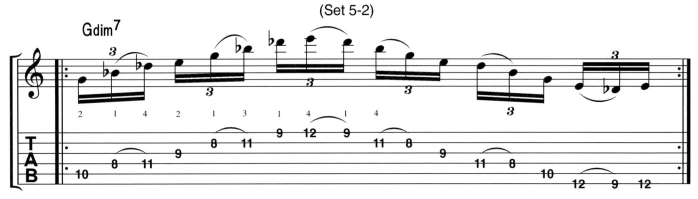

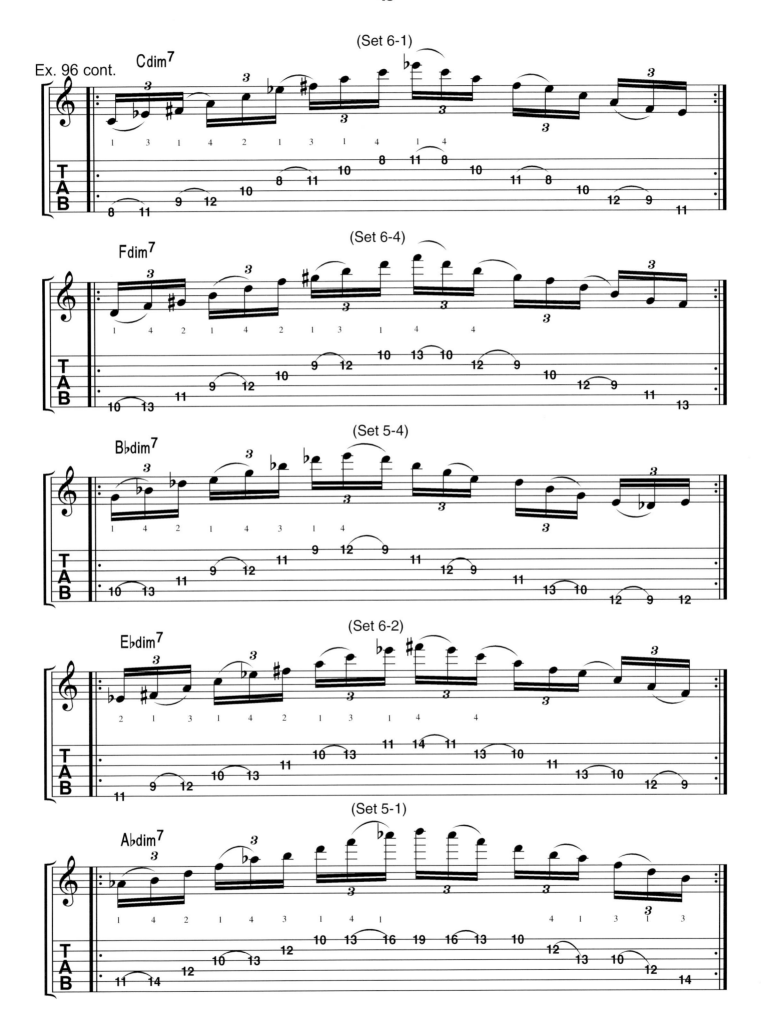

Ex. 96 cont.

practice suggestion #3

Expanding useability by practicing a given rhythmic phrase from each note in an arpeggio.

In this study, a one-measure rhythmic pattern is started from every note in the C7 arpeggio from SET 6-2. The resulting familiarity greatly increases control in using a given arpeggio pattern. Practice suggestion #3a shows practical application.

Play each measure twice to imprint into muscle memory, then move on to the next measure.

▶ **No. 62** (Ex. 97)

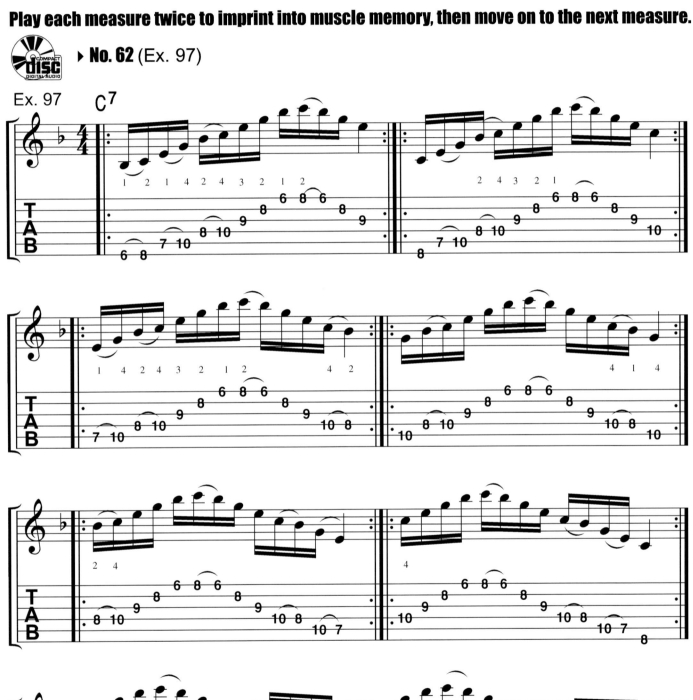

Ex. 97 cont.

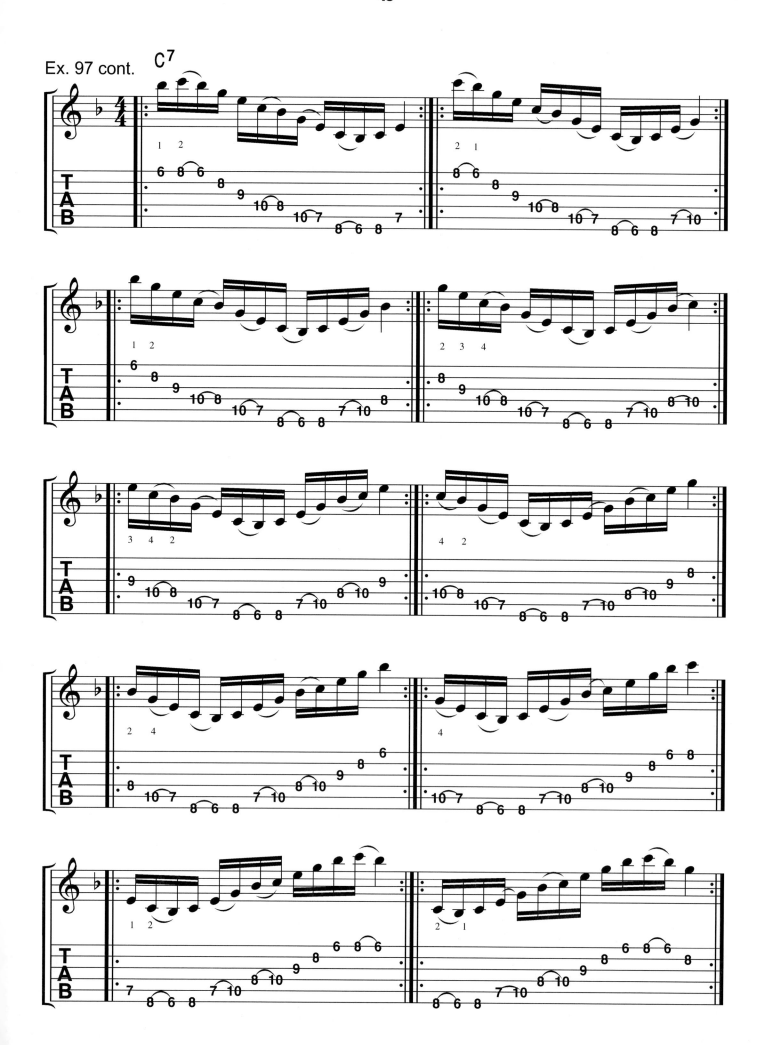

practice suggestion #3a

Applying the principal presented in practice suggestion #3 to a chord progression.

The point is...**learn to start your arpeggios from any note in the arpeggio!**

 No. 63 (Ex. 98)

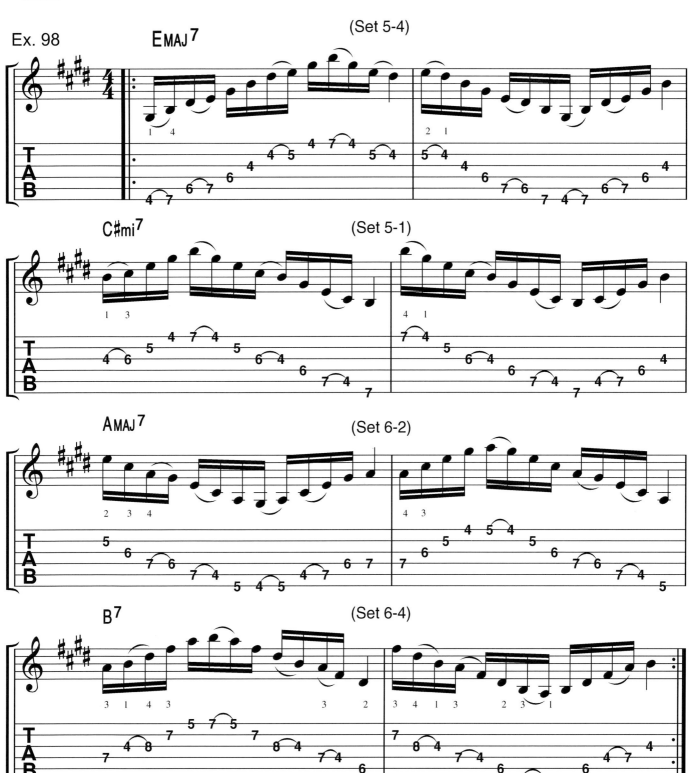

practice suggestion #4

The diatonic arpeggios of one key played consecutively, along the neck (using 5-2).

For this demonstration, the diatonic arpeggios in key of C Major are shown, using the fingerings of SET 5-2 exclusively. This same approach should be followed using the OTHER arpeggio sets as well, in this key and other keys.

▸ **No. 64** (Ex. 99)

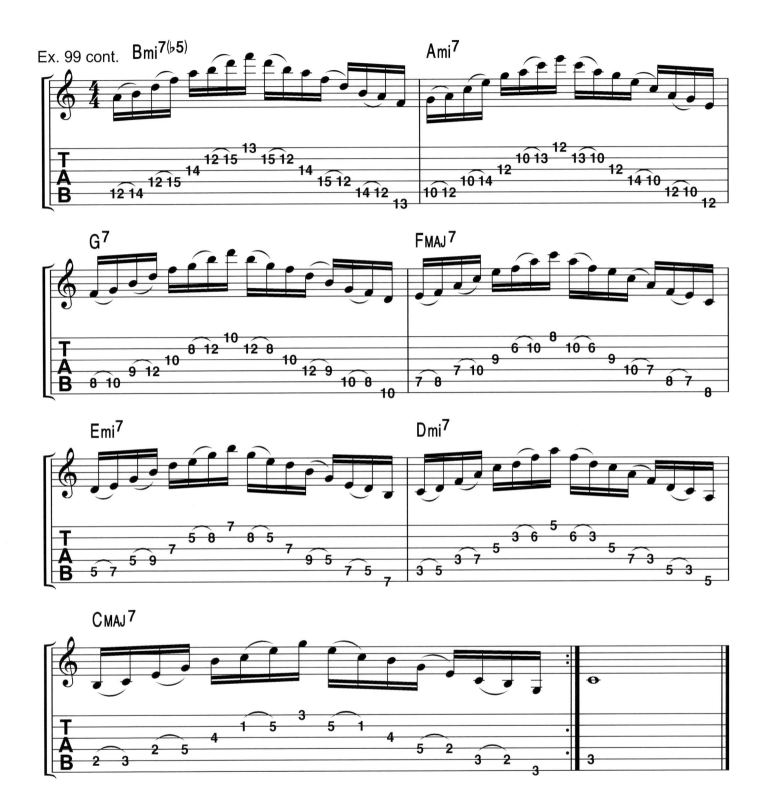

practice suggestion #4a

The diatonic arpeggios of one key played consecutively, along the neck (using set 5-1).

For this demonstration, the diatonic arpeggios in key of C Dorian (same as Bb Major) are shown, using the fingerings of SET 5-1 exclusively. This exercise can be applied to any key, ascending one arpeggio then descending the next.

▸ **No. 65** (Ex. 100)

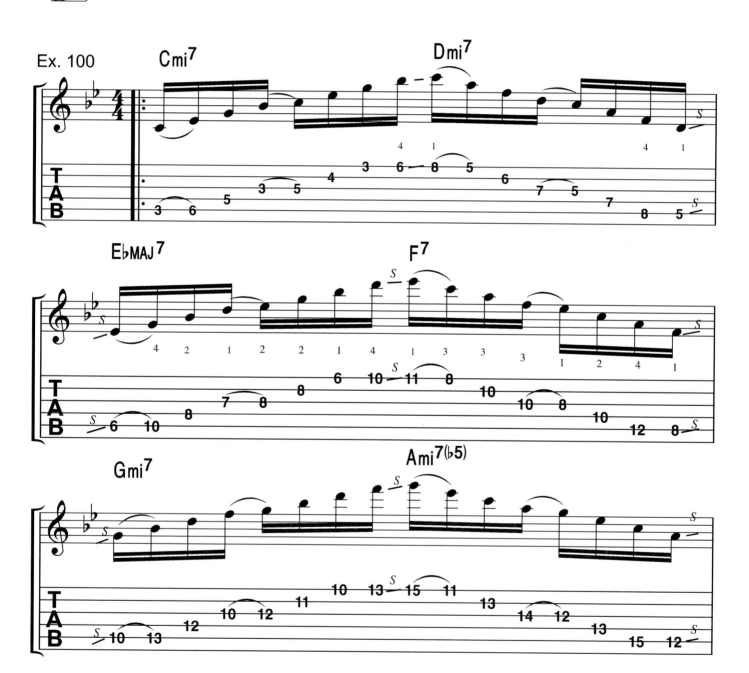

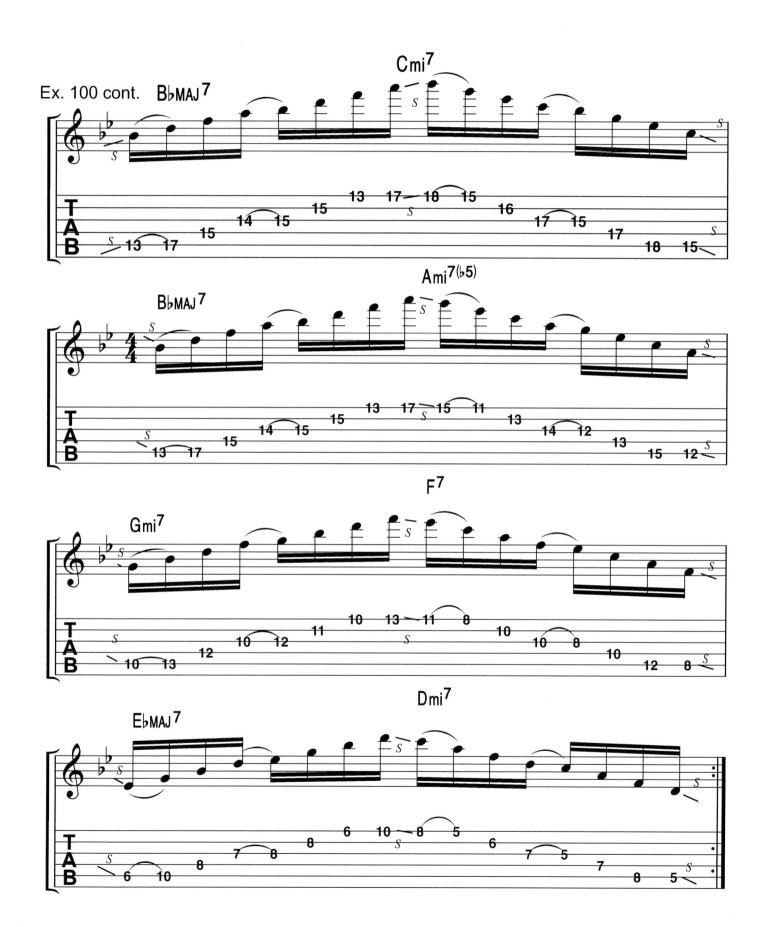

practice suggestion #5

Diatonic rapid-fire arpeggios of one key played consecutively, in one hand position.

This study demonstrates the diatonic arpeggios of the key of C Major played in one fretboard area. And, since there are 7 possible fingerings for each arpeggio, this progression could also be played in 6 other fingerings/locations for this same key!

▶ **No. 66** (Ex. 101)

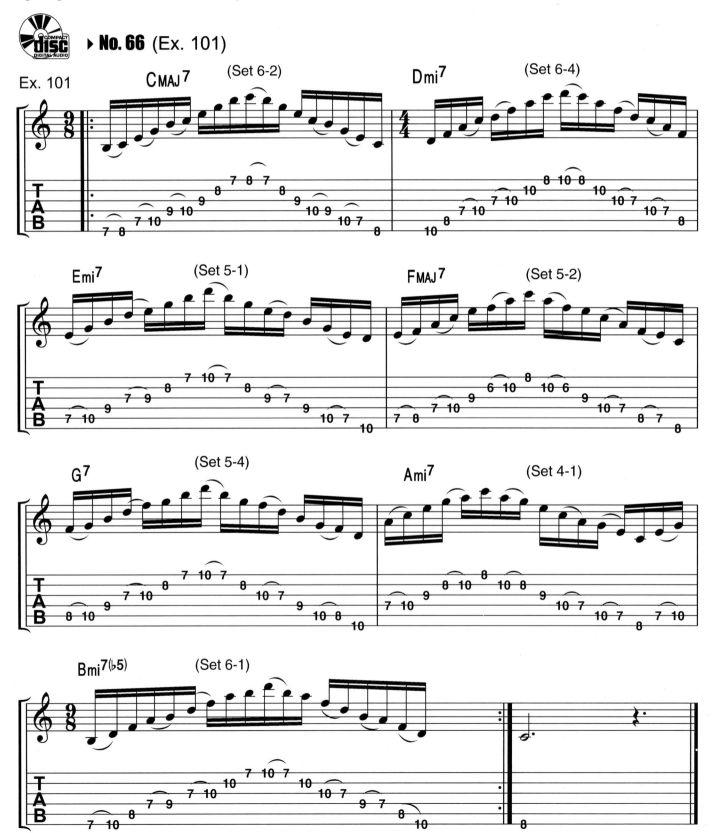

practice suggestion #6

Diatonic rapid-fire arpeggios of one key played non-consecutive order, in one position.

This study demonstrates the diatonic arpeggios of C Major played in the following order: I-vi-ii-V-iii-vi-IV-vii. This is a highly practical exercise, and an important complement to playing the arpeggios in consecutive order.

As with example No. 101, transfer this study to all fingerings in C major, & to all keys.

▶ **No. 67** (Ex. 102)

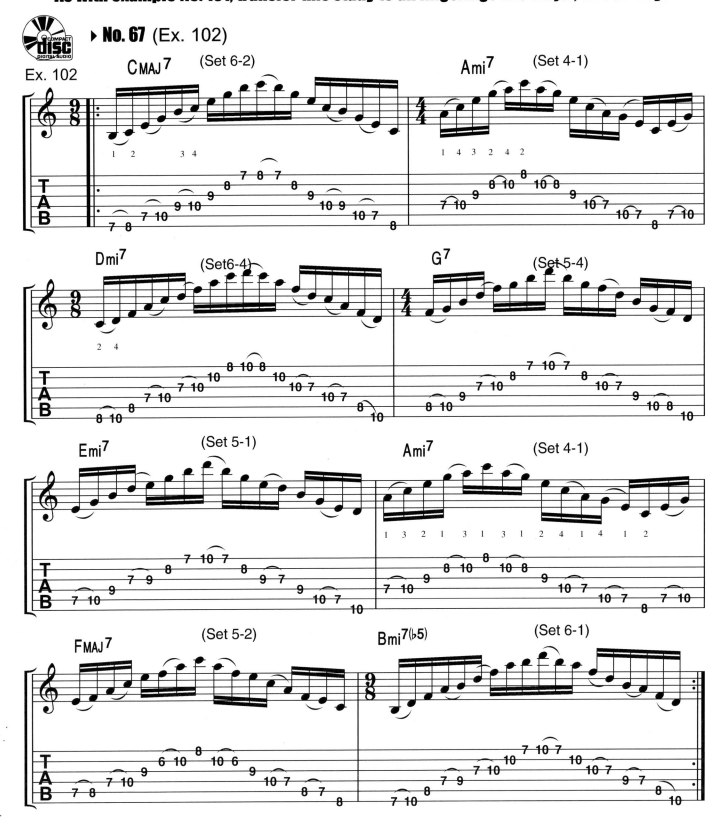

practice suggestion #7
Whole neck study connecting all seven arpeggios for one chord sound.

In order to sustain continuous motion that flows from one arpeggio position to the next, a bit of "creative connection" is required (occasionally the 9th is used as a passing note). Similar studies should be created for each arpeggio type.

All arpeggios in this study outline C Maj7.

▶ **No. 68** (Ex. 103)

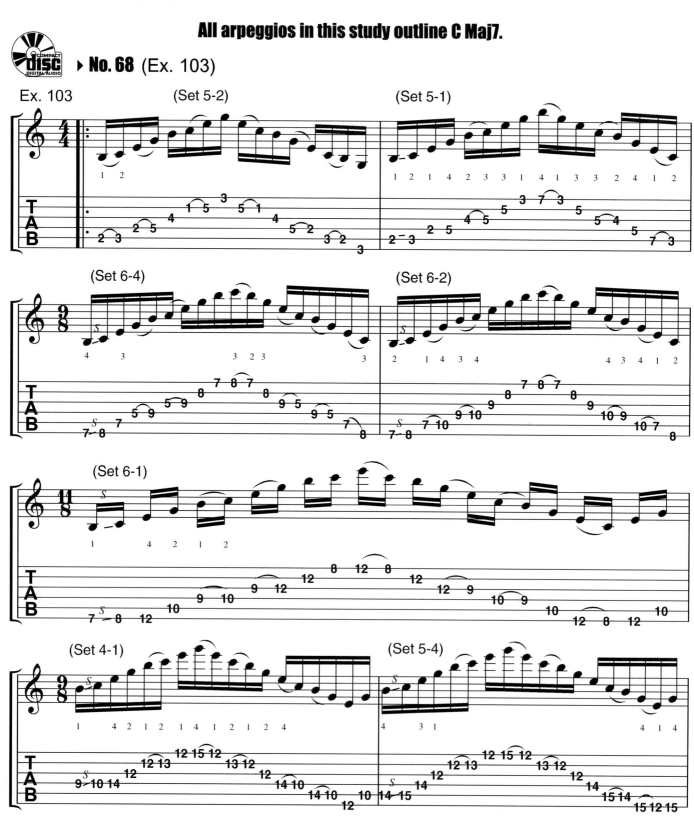

Ex. 103 cont.

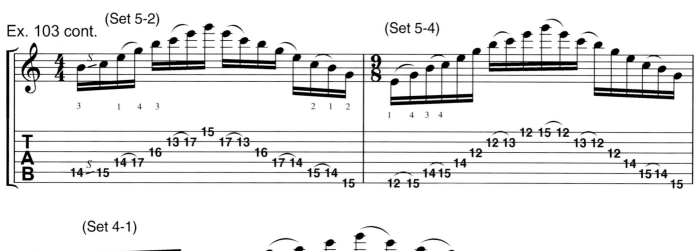

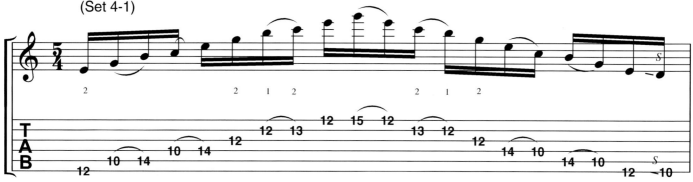

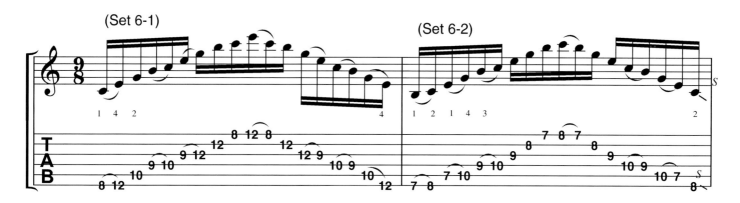

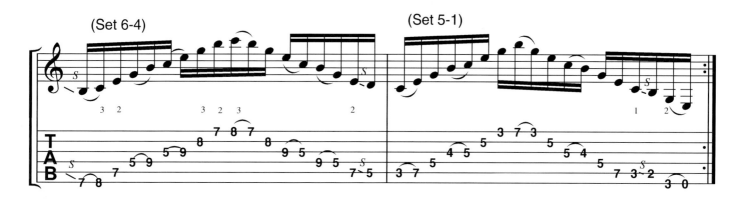

soloing etude no. 1

Study using rapid-fire arpeggios to outline each chord in a progression.

Chord Progression:
(16th note feel)

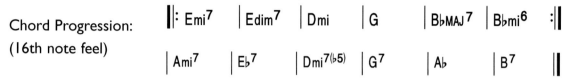

▶ **No. 69** (Ex. 104)

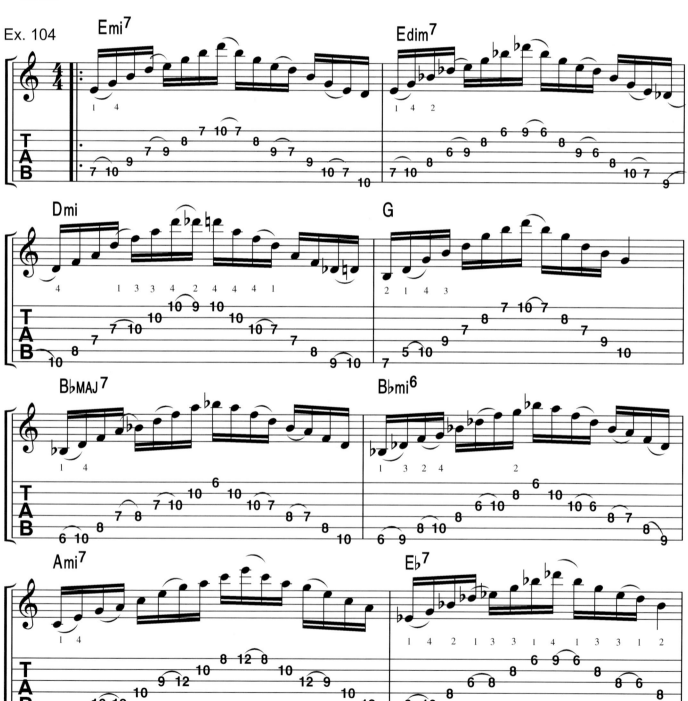

soloing etude no. 2

Demonstrating use of rapid-fire arpeggios over a 12-bar blues shuffle (Key of: A)

Chord Progression:

$$\|{:}\ A^7 \quad | D^7 \quad | A^7 \quad | A^7 \quad | D^7 \quad | D^7 \quad :\|$$

$$| A^7 \quad Bmi^7 \ | C\#mi^7\ Cmi^7 \ | E^9sus^4 \quad | Dmi^7 \quad | A^7 \quad D^7 \ | A^7 \quad E^7 \ \|$$

▶ **No. 70** (Ex. 105)

Ex. 105

soloing etude no. 3

Another study over the same chord progression that was used in etude no. 1.

This study is in a TRIPLET FEEL, and each arpeggio here begins with descending motion.

▶ **No. 71** (Ex. 106)

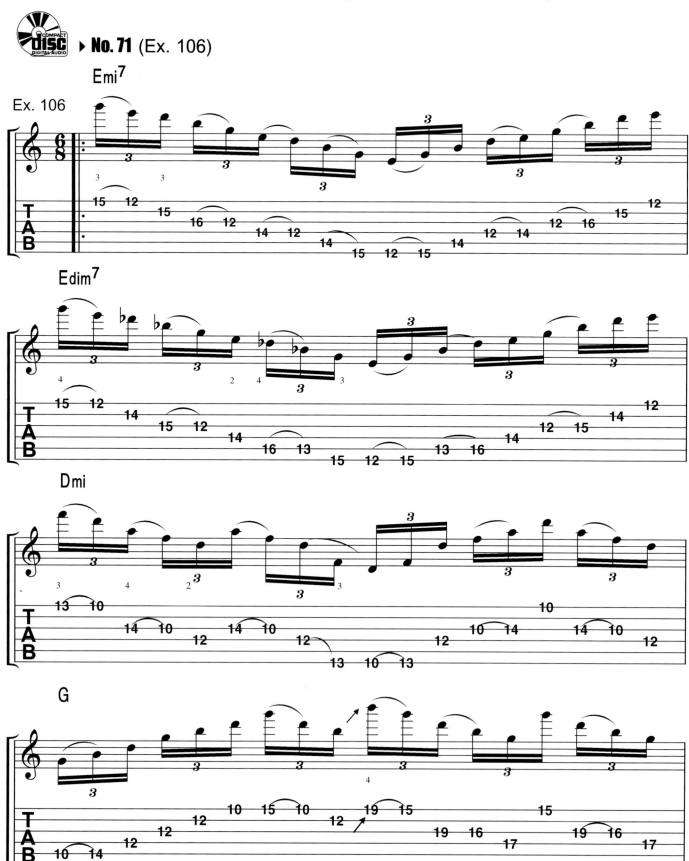

Ex. 106 cont.

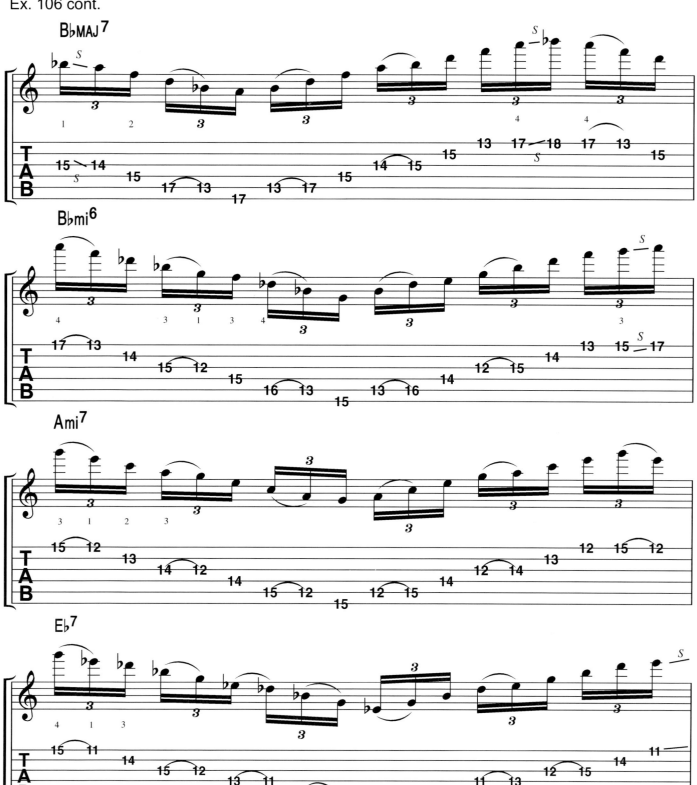

Ex. 106 cont.

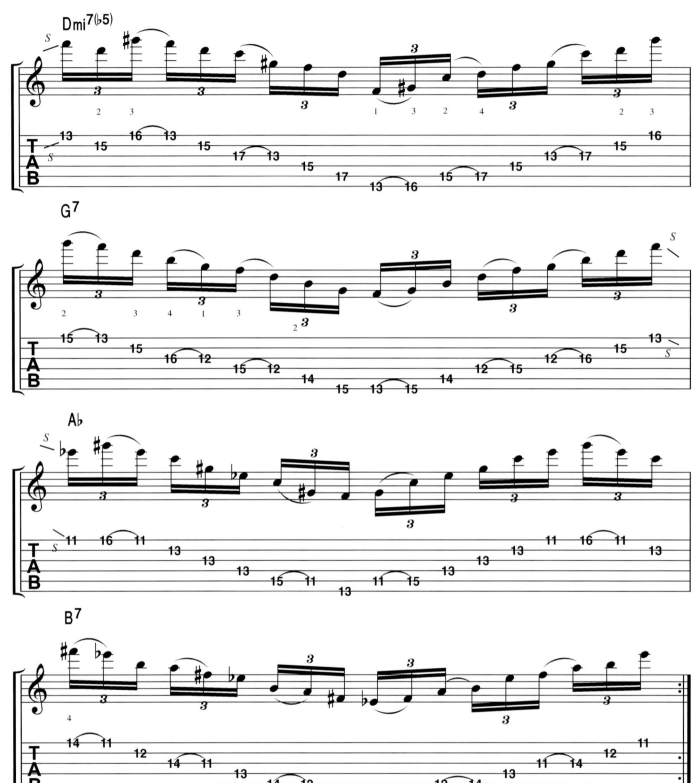

section two ▸ extended arpeggio runs
important points for study

▸ Extended Arpeggio Runs are <u>position-shifting</u> arpeggio exercises that cover a greater range of the fretboard than those presented in Section One. Each run is a repeating etude that uses predominantly the root, 3rd, 5th, and 7th of the arpeggio and *occasionally* a chord extension (i.e. the 6th, 9th, or 11th). These runs are fluid and flowing, facilitated by the use of slides, pull-offs, and hammers.

▸ Arpeggio runs are presented here for: **Minor 7, Dominant 7, Major 7, Diminished 7, Min. 7(♭5), Min. 6, Major Triadic,** and **Minor Triadic** applications.

▸ <u>These runs are organized into two groups:</u> one group demonstrating a 16th note feel in each run, and the second group demonstrating similar arpeggio runs with a triplet feel.

▸ Each exercise should be played continuously and repetitively, to develop non-thinking muscle memory and execution. It will be important to eventually **breakdown each run**, to isolate those 5-8 note sections that contain the sliding position shifts that get you from one arpeggio location to a different arpeggio location. These shifts demonstrate practical position shifting on the guitar, and should be integrated into your improvisation perhaps even more than should entire exercises.

▸ Try starting each run at its midway point, where the run begins its ascension. This greatly increases its usability and application.

▸ In order to play these studies at a fast tempo, the order of pickstrokes may need to be studied. *Strict alternate picking* (as explained in the appendix) means that each note is assigned a down or an upstroke from the start. A slide, hammer, or pull-off simply replaces a pickstroke, but does not change the predetermined assignment. A complete understanding of this is helpful (see appendix).

outline for this chapter

Arpeggio Runs with a 16th Note Feel

minor 7th arpeggio runs
Play each line repetitively.

As you practice these studies, always be aware of the non-shifting rapid-fire arpeggio patterns that these studies are connecting. These arpeggio runs move from one non-shifting arpeggio pattern into the next, weaving together the patterns learned in the first section of this book.

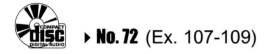

▸ **No. 72** (Ex. 107-109)

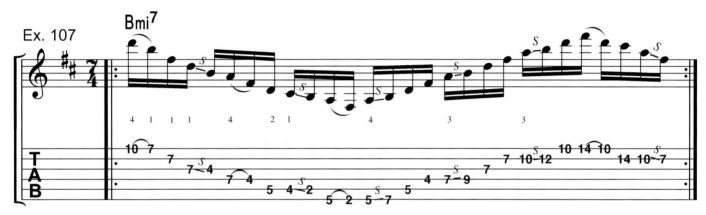

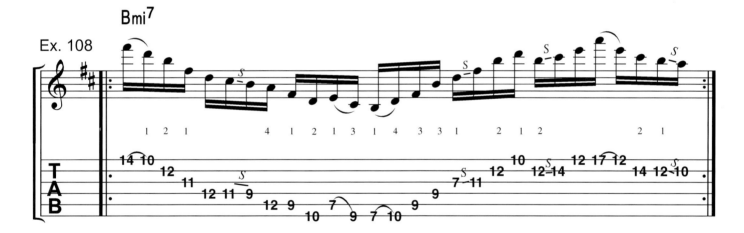

dominant 7th arpeggio runs (16ths)

Play each line repetitively.

 No. 73 (Ex. 110-112)

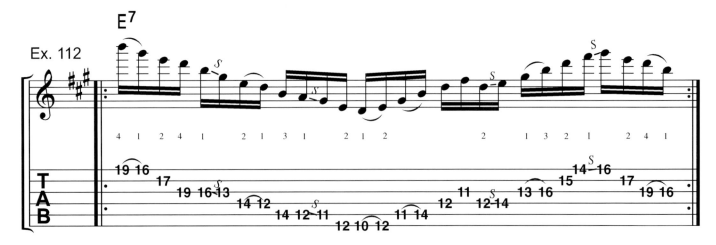

major 7th arpeggio runs (16ths)

Play each line repetitively.

 ▶ **No. 74** (Ex. 113-115)

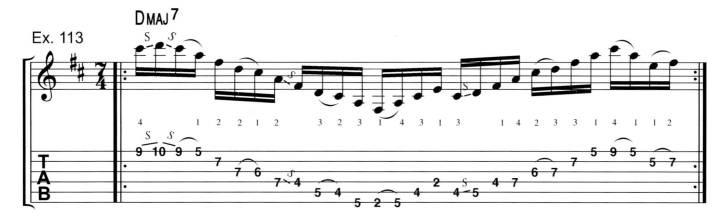

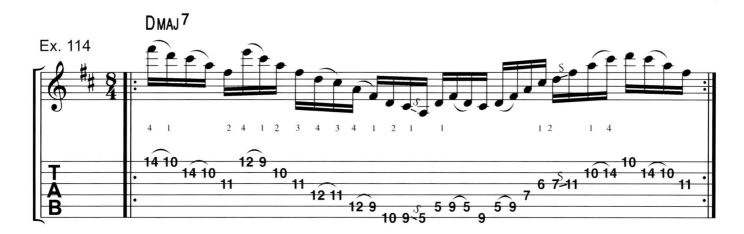

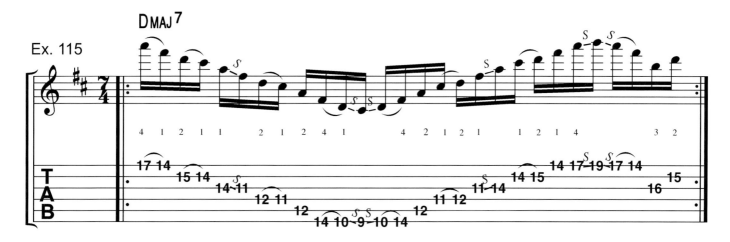

diminished 7th arpeggio runs (16ths)

Play each line repetitively.

As you practice these studies, always be aware of the non-shifting rapid-fire arpeggio patterns that these studies are connecting. These arpeggio runs move from one non-shifting arpeggio pattern into the next, weaving together the patterns learned in the first section of this book.

 ▶ **No. 75** (Ex. 116-118)

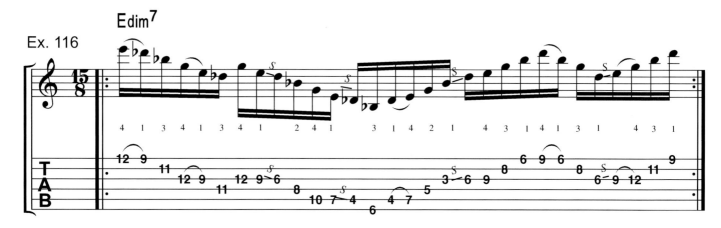

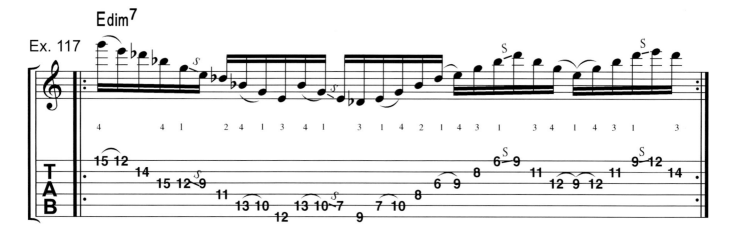

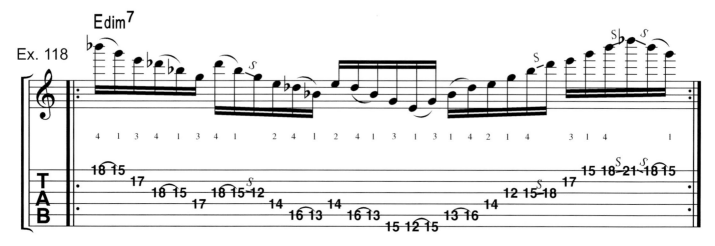

minor7(♭5) arpeggio runs (16ths)

Minor7(♭5) is also known as "half-diminished" or ⌀.

C#min7(♭5) contains the same notes as A9, Emi6 and GMajor7(♭5), so these runs will work over those chords as well!

▶ **No. 76** (Ex. 119-121)

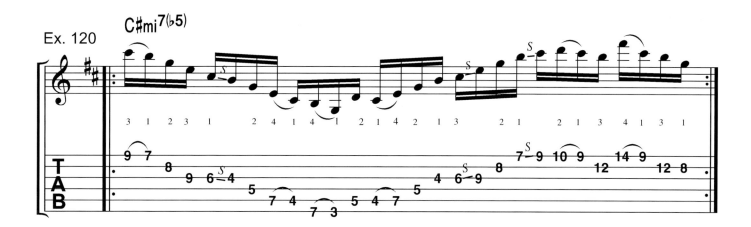

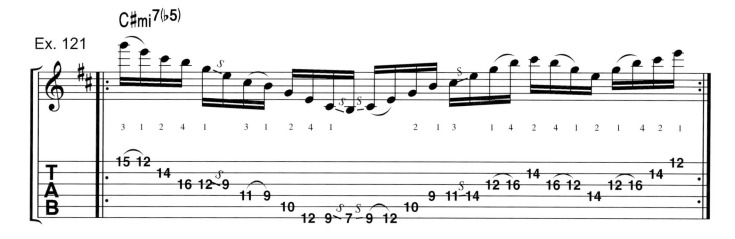

minor 6th arpeggio runs (16ths)

Emi6 contains the same notes as C♯mi7(♭5), A9, and GMajor7(♭5) so these runs will work over those chords as well!

 **No. 77** (Ex. 122-124)

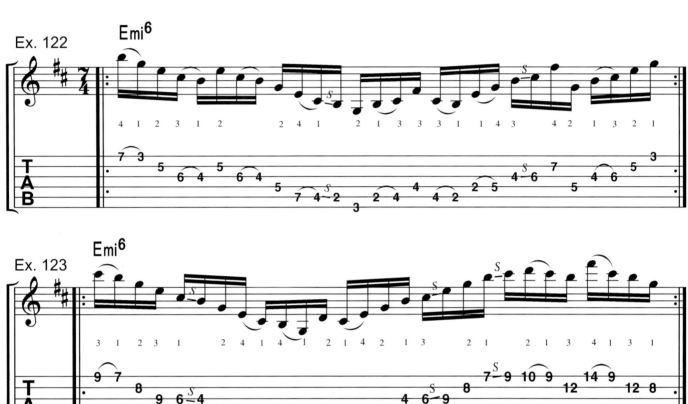

You may have noticed that these runs are identical to those presented on the previous page for C♯mi7(♭5). C♯mi7(♭5) and Emi6 contain the same notes, but it is still very important to be able to readily identify pathways of arpeggio motion by thinking of the given chord root. For this reason, the student should come to recognize these runs as being associated with either the "C♯" or "E" root note, respective locators for starting arpeggio runs on either the C♯mi7(♭5) or Emi6 chord.

major triad arpeggio runs (16ths)

Play each line repetitively.

▶ **No. 78** (Ex. 125-127)

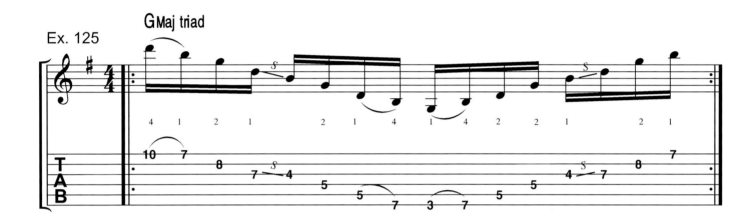

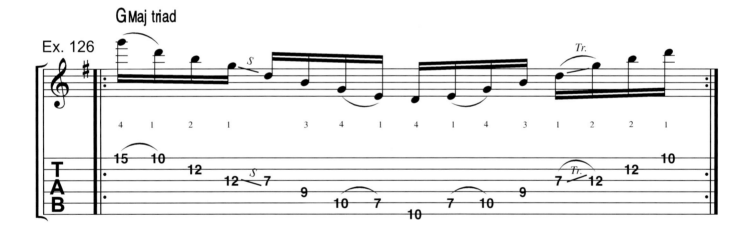

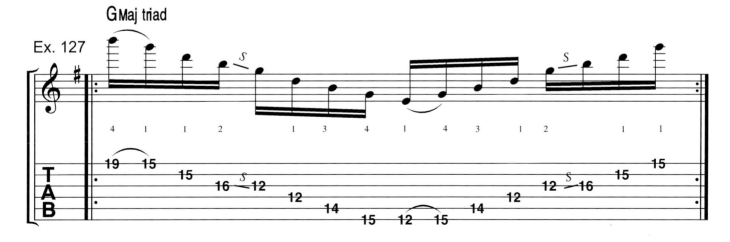

minor triad arpeggio runs (16ths)

Play each line repetitively.

 ▶ **No. 79** (Ex. 128-130)

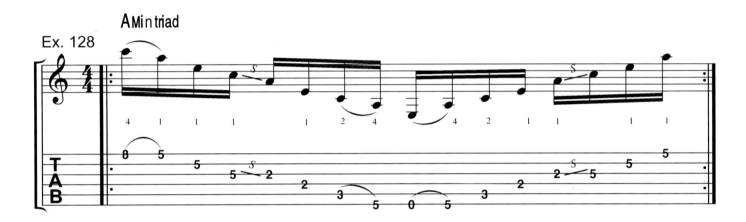

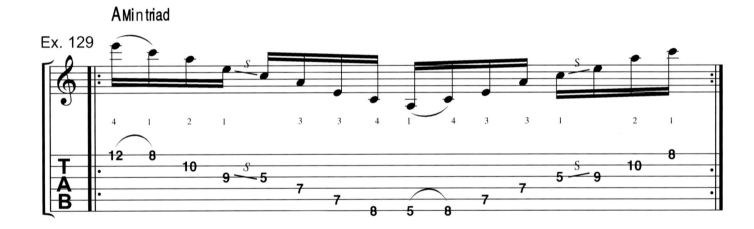

Arpeggio Runs with a Triplet Feel

minor 7th arpeggio runs (triplets)

Play each line repetitively

 ▸ **No. 80** (Ex. 131-133)

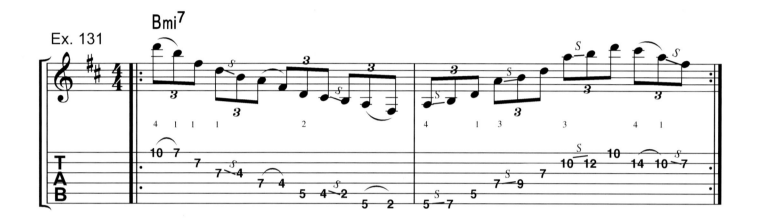

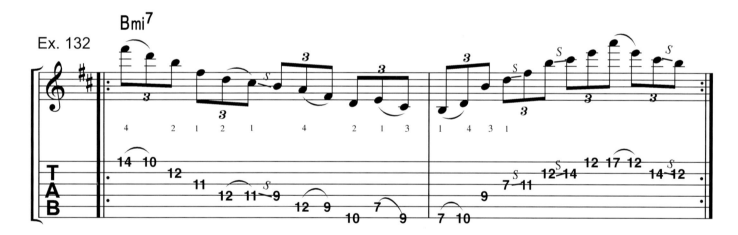

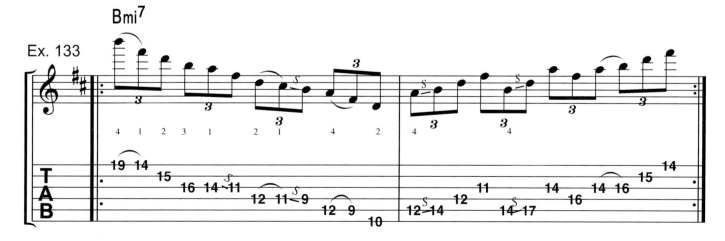

dominant 7th arpeggio runs (triplets)

Play each line repetitively

▸ **No. 81** (Ex. 134-136)

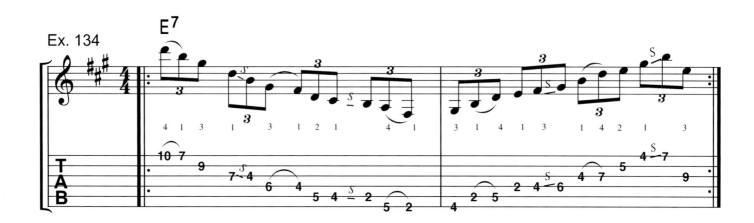

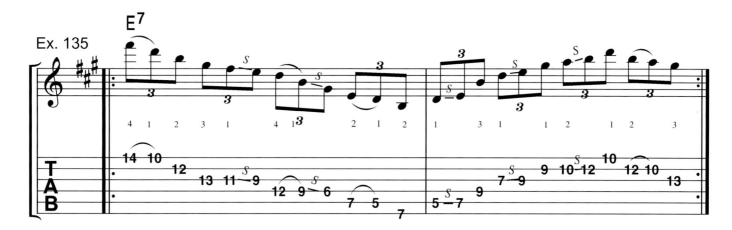

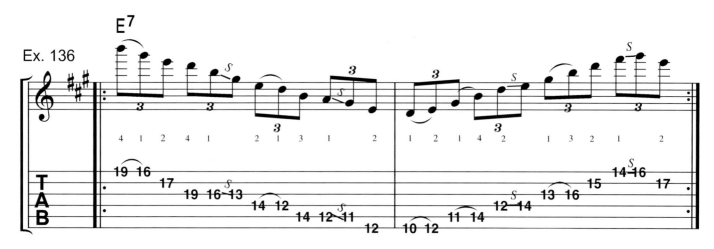

major 7th arpeggio runs (triplets)
Play each line repetitively

 ▸ **No. 82** (Ex. 137-139)

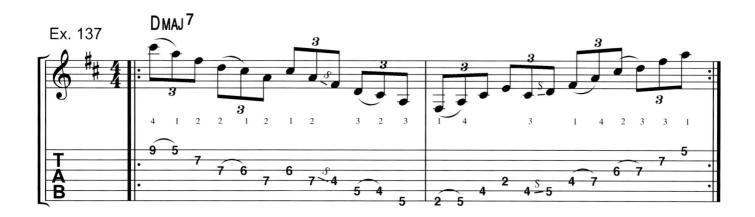

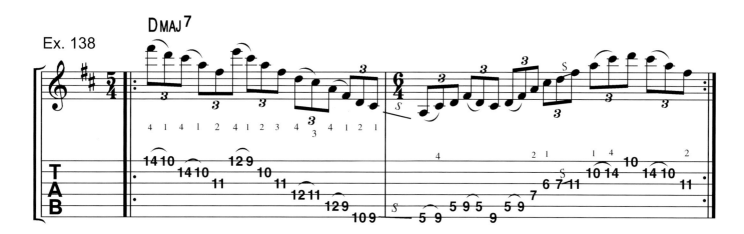

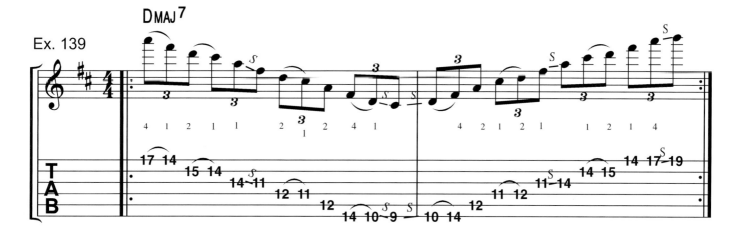

diminished 7th arpeggio runs (triplets)
Play each line repetitively

 ▸ **No. 83** (Ex. 140-142)

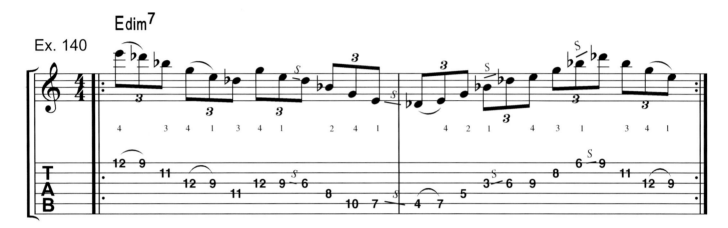

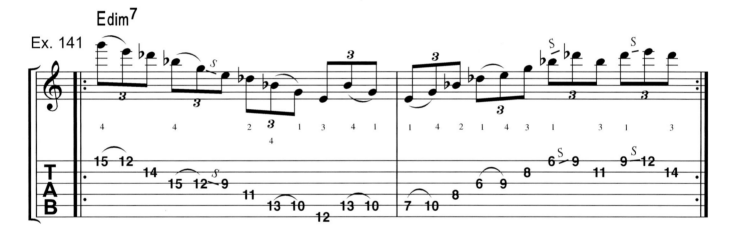

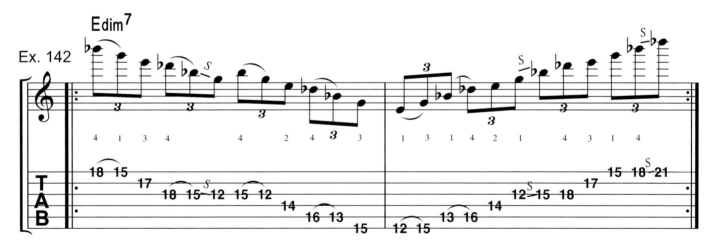

minor7(♭5) arpeggio runs (triplets)

Minor7(♭5) is also known as "half-diminished" or ∅.

C♯min7(♭5) contains the same notes as A9, Emi6 and GMajor7(♭5), so these runs will work over those chords as well!

 ▸ **No. 84** (Ex. 143-145)

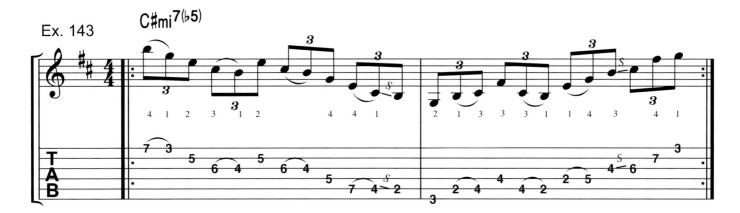

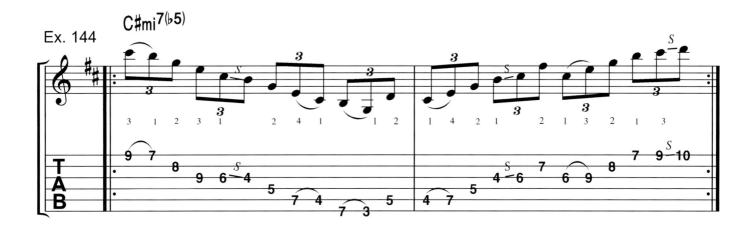

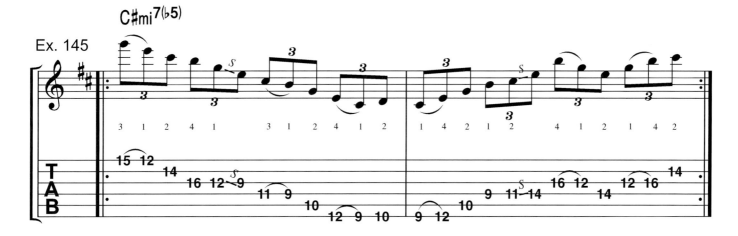

minor 6th arpeggio runs (triplets)

Emi6 contains the same notes as C#mi7(♭5), A9, and GMajor(♭5) so these runs will work over those chords as well!

 ▶ **No. 85** (Ex. 146-148)

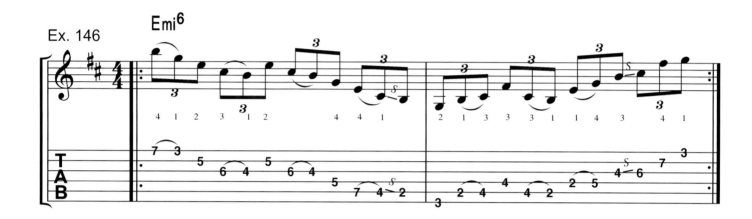

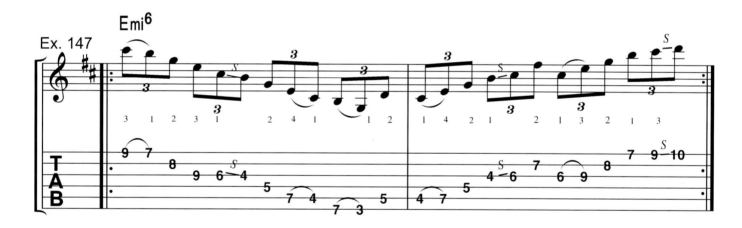

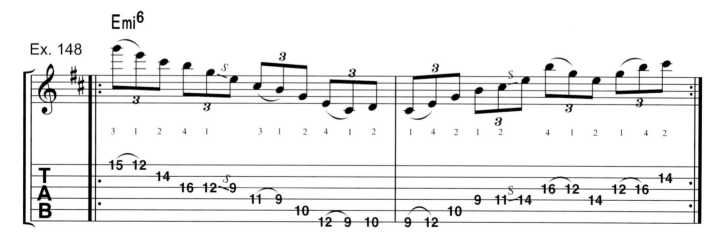

major triad arpeggio runs (triplets)

Play each line repetitively.

 No. 86 (Ex. 149-151)

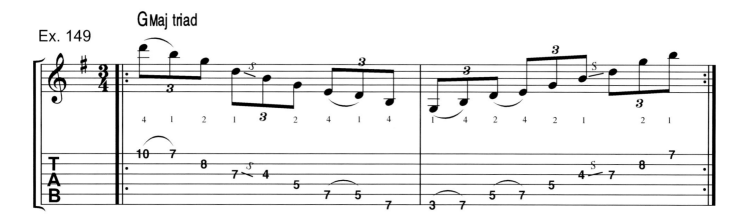

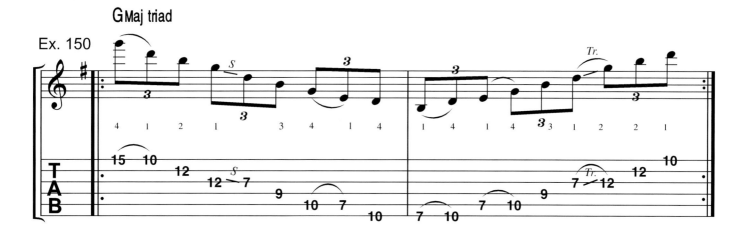

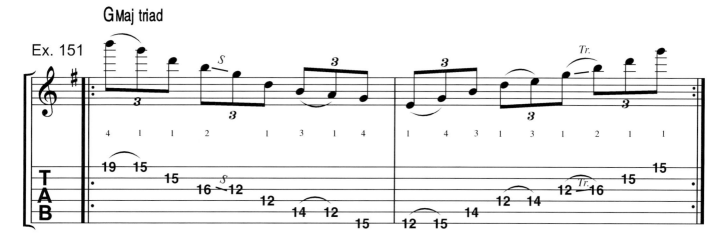

minor triad arpeggio runs (triplets)

Play each line repetitively.

 **No. 87** (Ex. 152-154)

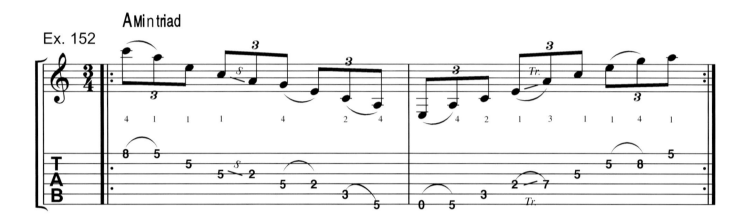

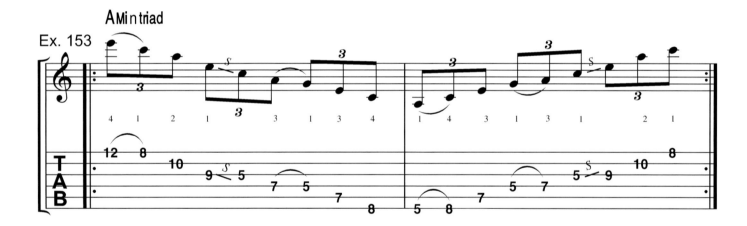

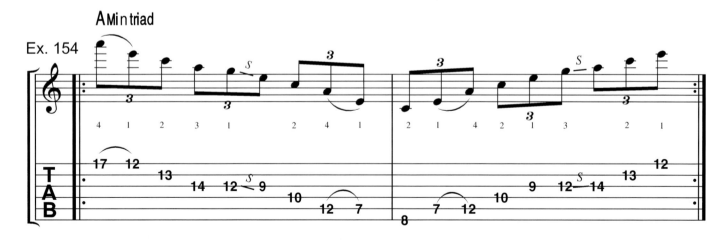

soloing etudes & practice suggestions
(using extended arpeggio runs and rapid-fire arpeggios)

practice suggestion #8

Exercises for connecting rapid-fire arpeggios & extended arpeggio runs over one chord (Bmi7)

In these exercises, all arpeggios and arpeggio runs outline a Bmi7 chord, using a 16th note feel. The student should follow similar procedure for Dom. 7, Maj. 7, dim. 7, mi7(b5), min. 6, Maj. triad and Min. triad arpeggios.

All arpeggios and runs in these studies outline a Bmi7 chord.

 ▶ **No. 88** (Ex. 155)

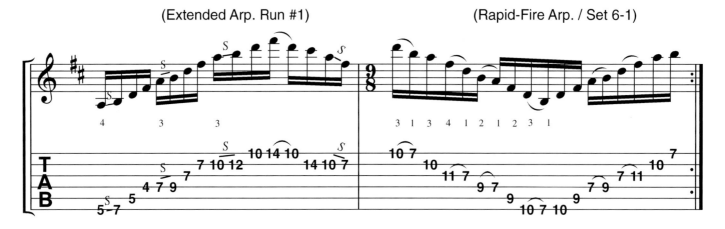

practice suggestion #9

Exercises for connecting rapid-fire arpeggios & extended arpeggio runs over one chord (GMaj7)

In these exercises, all arpeggios and arpeggio runs outline a GMaj7 chord, using a triplet feel. The student should follow similar procedure for Min. 7, Dom. 7, dim. 7, min. 7(♭5), min. 6, Maj. triad and Min. triad arpeggios.

All arpeggios and runs in these studies outline a GMaj7 chord.

▸ **No. 91** (Ex. 158)

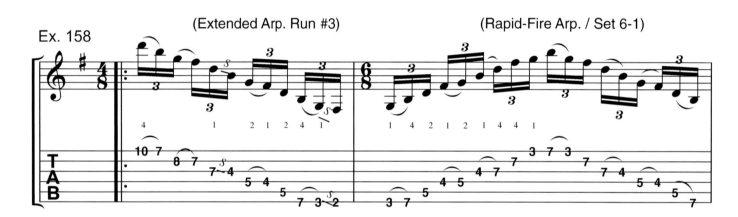

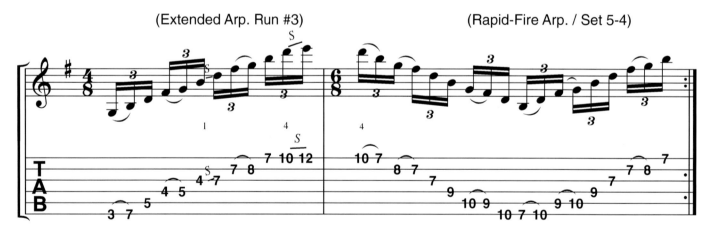

soloing etude no. 4

Harmonic outlining using extended arpeggio runs and rapid-fire arpeggios.

Chord Progression: ‖: EMAJ⁷ | AMAJ⁷ | C♯mi⁷ | D⁷ :‖

▶ **No. 94** (Ex. 161)

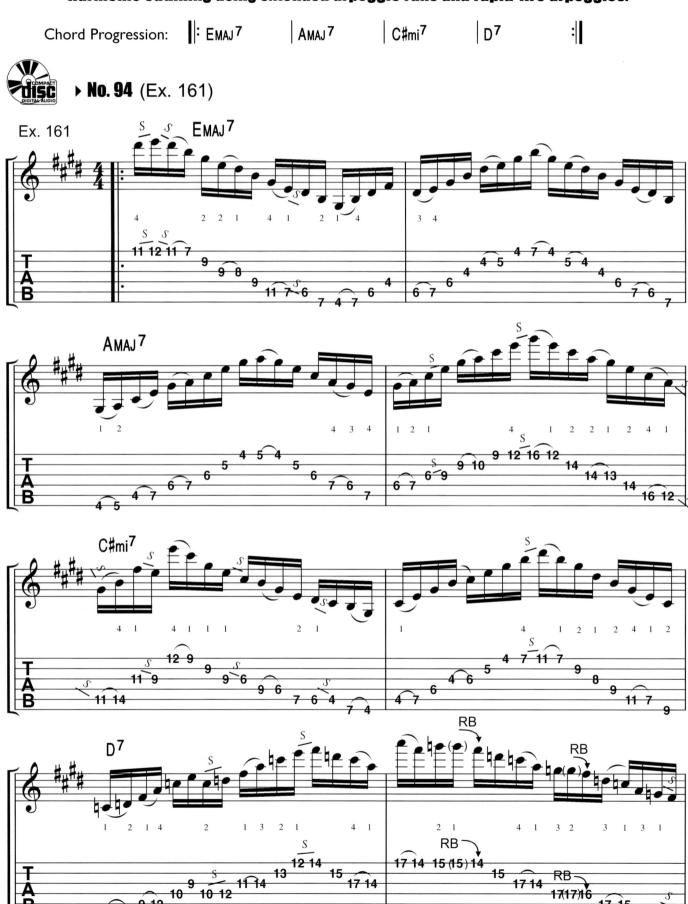

Ex. 161 cont.

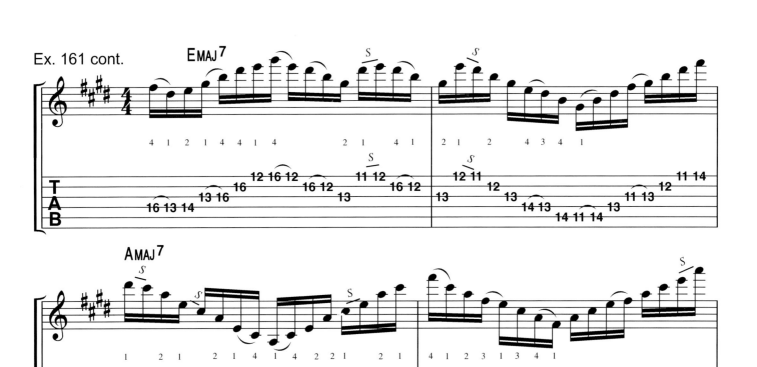

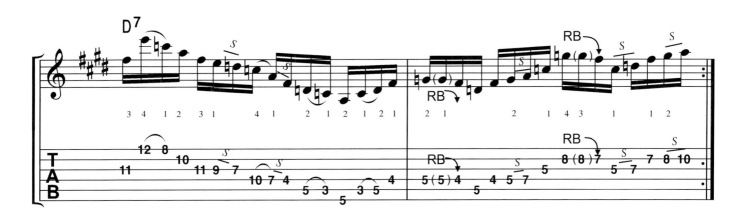

soloing etude no. 5

Harmonic outlining, using extended arpeggio runs and rapid-fire arpeggios.

This study uses the following chord progression:

$\|:$ Ami $\quad|$ G#dim^7 $|$ G $\quad|$ $\frac{D}{F\#}$ $\quad|$ $\frac{Dmi}{F}$ $\quad|$ $\frac{Ami}{E}$ $|$ F $\quad|$ Bdim^7 $:\|$

▸ **No. 95** (Ex. 162)

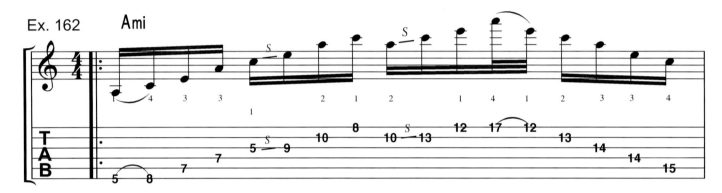

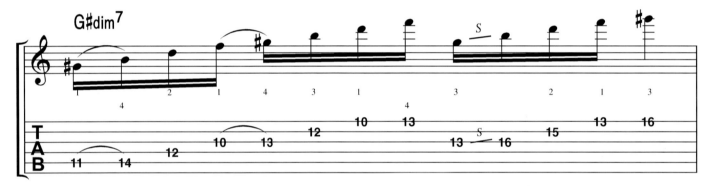

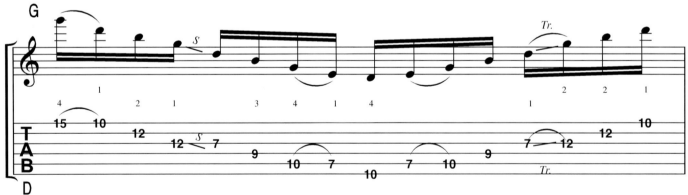

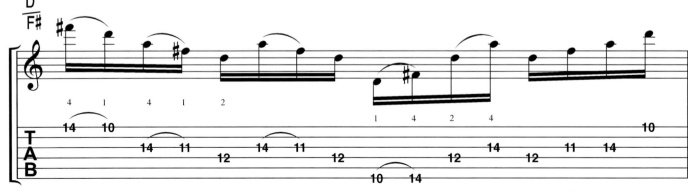

Ex. 162 cont.

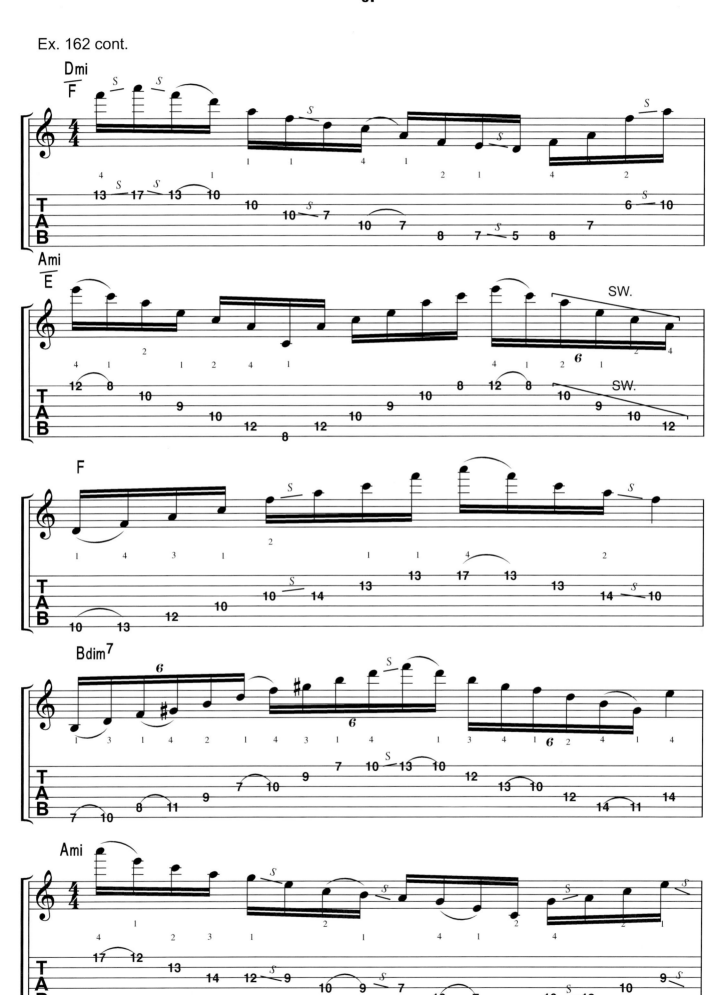

Ex. 162 cont.

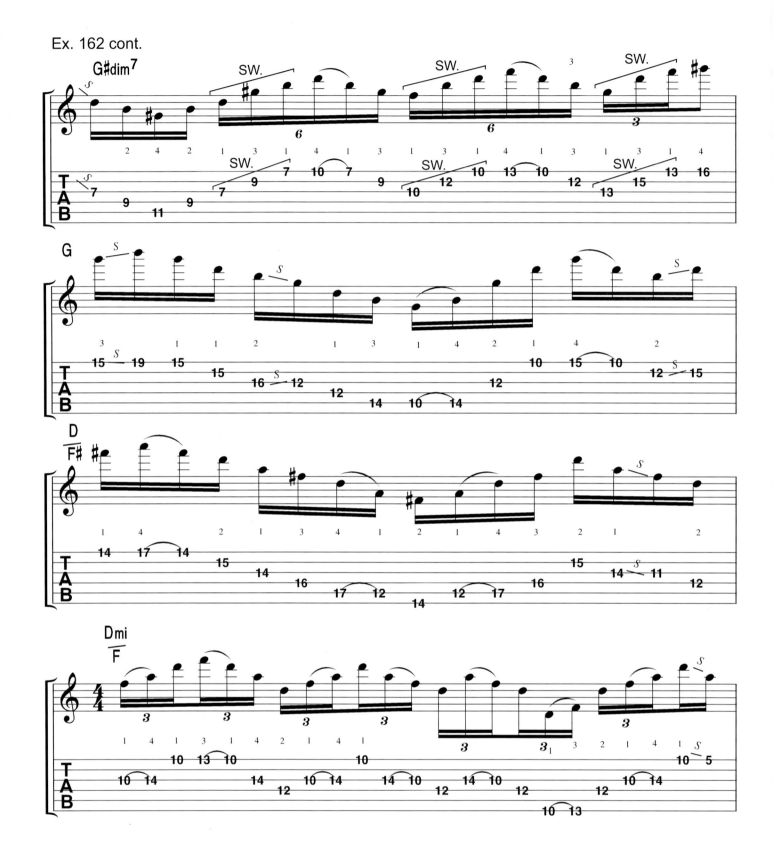

Ex. 162 cont.

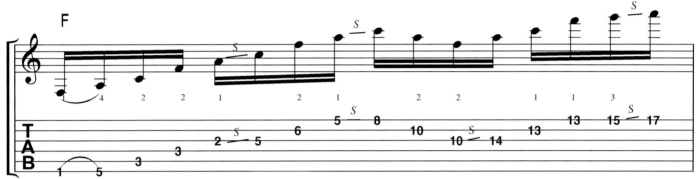

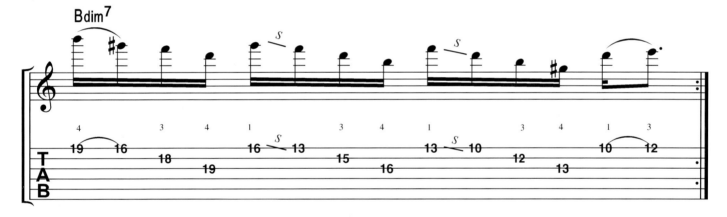

soloing etude no. 6 (comprehensive)

Combining minor 7th arpeggio runs with Hendrix style chord-melody (from Book 3).

Play this study repetitively over the following chord progression:

All runs and licks outline an Emi7 chord, but work against all chords in the progression (typical of minor pent. soloing).

▸ **No. 96** (Ex. 163)

Ex. 163

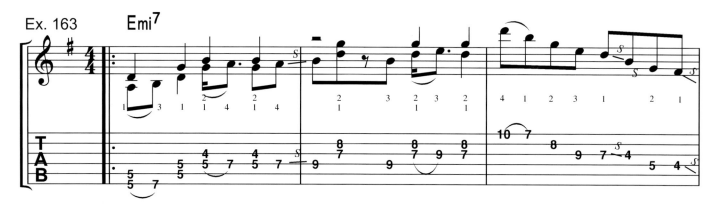

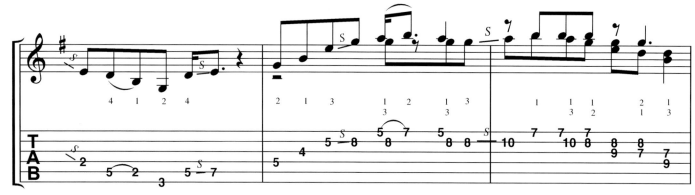

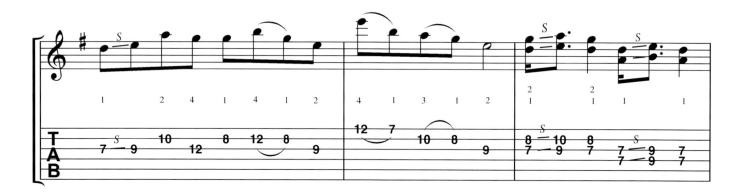

Ex. 163 cont.

soloing etude no. 7 (comprehensive)

Combining techniques from this book & other books in the series, to create fluid motion.

Chord progression:

No. 97 (Ex. 164)

Ex. 164

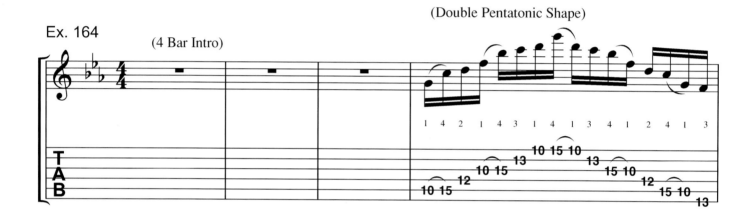

(4 Bar Intro)

(Double Pentatonic Shape)

(Horizontal Pentatonic Motion)

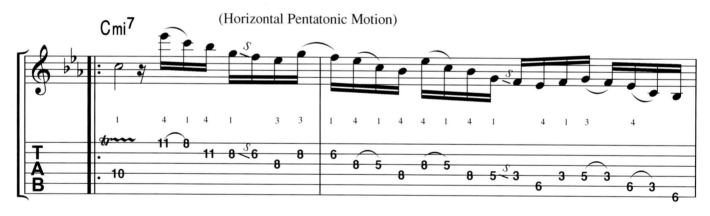

Cmi7

Cmi7

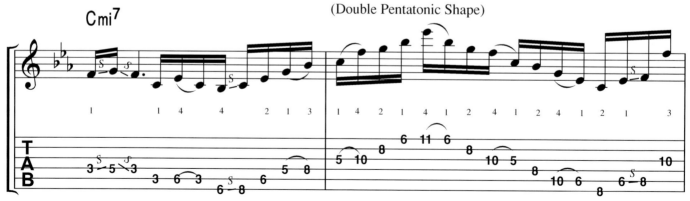

(Double Pentatonic Shape)

Cmi7

Ex. 164 cont.

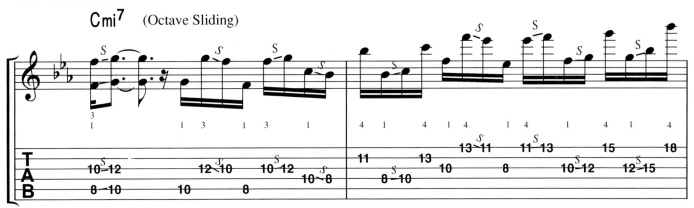

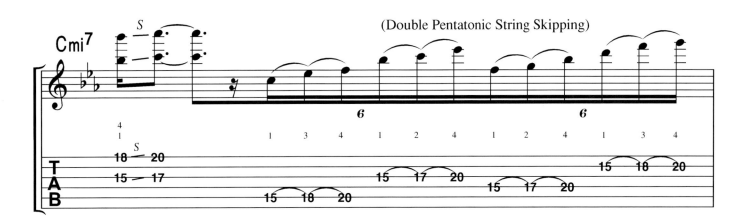

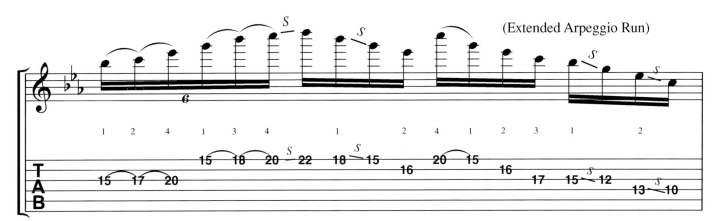

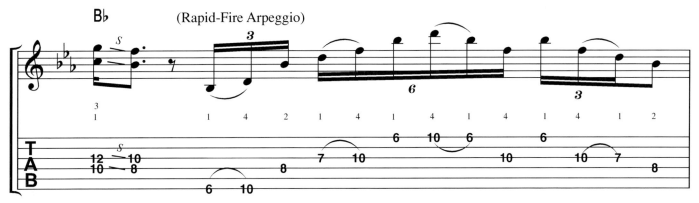

Ex. 164 cont.

(Hendrix Style Chord-Melody)

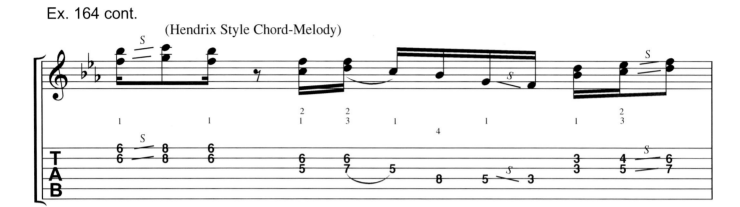

(Rapid-Fire Arpeggio)

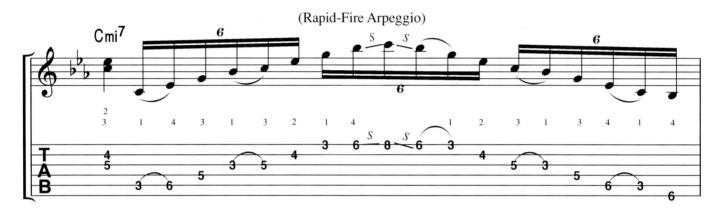

(Wide Interval Arpeggios)   (Rapid-Fire Arpeggio)

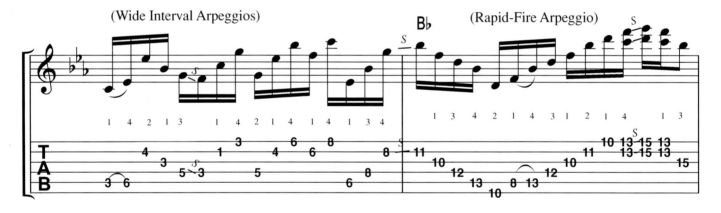

(Horizontal Pentatonic Motion)

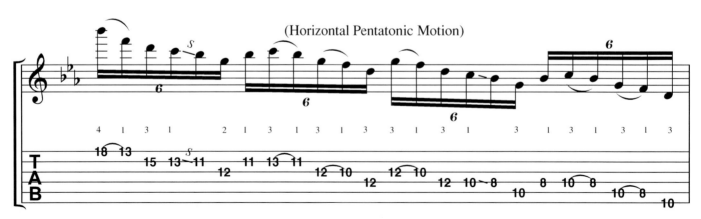

Ex. 164 cont.

appendix

Guidelines for using this book

Developing Muscle Memory

This book consists of melodic patterns that are designed to increase the guitarist's ability to play fluid, continuous streams of notes that harmonically outline specific chords by using arpeggios. Virtuosic fretboard control is largely the result of *muscle memory*, when memorized finger patterns are so familiar they can be played almost effortlessly. This gives a guitarist the mental freedom to listen to what he is playing and create music, rather than trying to continually remember where his fingers are supposed to go next.

In developing muscle memory, initial study and memorization should be very deliberate, with careful intellectual attention given to the execution of each and every note in a given study. First, memorize a study. Then, practice it frequently with a metronome at **ultra-slow speeds!** (as in one note-per-click with the metronome on 76 bpm)! While this may seem tedious, it will imprint the intellectual control of the pattern into your mind and hands. This slow-motion imprinting is crucial to developing blazing fluidity and freedom, which will come later. It doesn't happen overnight, but rather over a period of months, as a particular pattern is practiced continually and carefully.

As you practice an exercise at extremely slow tempos, practice looking ahead...to the next group of notes in the study, even as your fingers are occupied with executing the notes of the moment. This is the psychological aspect of musicianship which is often overlooked and underdeveloped...the ability to focus the mental attention either directly on the notes of the moment, or to look ahead to the next group of notes mentally while the fingers rely on muscle memory to execute the notes of the moment. *Consciously develop the mental habit of looking ahead to the upcoming notes.* Each study should be memorized and played repetitively on a daily basis (at both fast and slow tempos) for a period of months, as this will develop muscle memory.

The Rhythm of Continual Motion...16th's & Triplets

Each exercise in this series of books is designed for repetition, so that it starts over again and again without breaking the flow of continual motion. This format is ideal for establishing muscle memory with new and unfamiliar finger patterns. Most examples are constructed in *either 16th notes or triplets--the two fundamental rhythmic figures for rapid, streaming melodic flow.*

A wide variety of time signatures are used in this series of books: 4/4, 5/4, 6/4, 7/4, 8/4, 6/8, 7/8, 9/8, 12/8, and 15/8. This is nothing to be concerned about, and you really don't even need to pay much attention to it. Grasping control of either a 16th-note feel or triplet motion is the primary requisite for being able to apply these exercises to your own music making, no matter what type of groove you are playing over. The unusual time signatures were simply a mathematical necessity, used to accommodate the wide variety of sequential melodic patterns, which may be in formulated in groups of 3, 4, 5, 6, or 7 notes (or sometimes even larger sequential groupings). The goal is simply to be able to play any given exercise in a continuous stream of either 16th notes or triplets.

The Concept of Strict Alternate Picking

In executing slow passages, it is often not necessary to observe any rules in picking. However, when executing fast runs on guitar, it is very helpful to have an organized approach to picking, and among the best guitarists, there *IS* a system which is used more often than not. In its simplest description, strict alternate picking applies to streams of notes in a continuous rhythm, where the first note is struck with a downstroke, the second with an upstroke, etc., maintaining strict alternation. There are two reasons why it is wise to develop alternate picking:

1) **It makes efficient use of picking hand movements,** which allows for execution of high speed passages; and

2) **It develops a natural inclination to use either a downstroke or an upstroke for each note based on which part of the beat the note falls on,** which results in a consistent approach to picking notes a certain way, depending on how they feel rhythmically, (as opposed to haphazard random picking). For example, continuous eighth notes would be picked down-up-down-up, which puts the downstroke on the first half of the beat, and the upstroke on the second half.

Notice that when you verbally count out loud (either eighth notes, sixteenth notes, or triplets), *placing a slightly harder verbal accent on the first part of every beat helps you feel the rhythm internally.* So it goes with picking. Strict alternate picking uses a downstroke at the beginning of each beat (*except in picking triplets), which makes musical sense, because the downstroke naturally has a slightly heavier attack than the upstroke. Place a slight accent (>) at the beginning of each beat when picking continuous streams of notes.

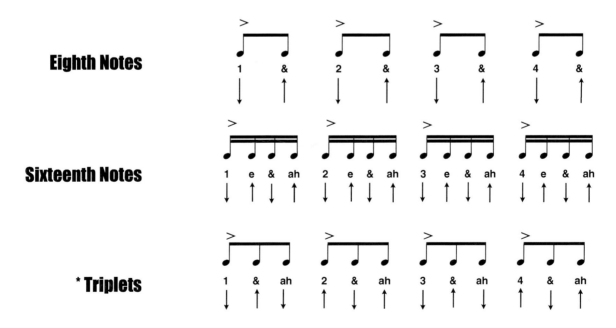

*(In picking triplets, the first and third beats start with a downstroke, the second and fourth beats start with an upstroke. Learn to place the accent at the start of every triplet, whether using a downstroke or an upstroke.)

Strict Alternate Picking with Hammers, Pulls, & Slides

Finally, we must address what happens to the order of downstrokes and upstrokes when a particular note does not require a pickstroke, as in when a hammer-on, pull-off, or a slide is used. When this is the case (as it often is in the studies presented in this book), the following rule applies: **A SLIDE, HAMMER, PULL-OFF, OR BEND WILL** *REPLACE* **THE PICKSTROKE WITHIN THE ASSIGNED PICKING ORDER.**

For example, in a group of four sixteenth notes where there is a slide from the second to the third note, the picking order would be down-up-slide-up. The third note is sounded by the fretting hand sliding to it, so the pick would move down above the string without touching it, while the fretting hand slides to the note, thus maintaining the organization of the picking order and the rhythmic feel. Another example could be given in picking a series of triplets where there is a hammer from the first to the second note in each triplet. Here, the picking order would be down-hammer-down, up-hammer-up, down-hammer-down, up-hammer-up.

To develop this practical approach to picking, first learn to play a given exercise without any slides, hammers, or pull-offs, so that every note is picked. Remember, it is down-up-down-up for sixteenth notes, or down-up-down/up-down-up for triplets. Also, don't forget to place an accent on the first note of each beat. Get used to the way the picking feels with strict alternation, picking every note. Then go back and eliminate those pick strokes that are actually replaced by the slides, hammers, or pulls (on these notes, the pick makes a "phantom stroke", moving over the string without hitting it). In the initial stages of applying this picking approach to a given passage, *use an exaggerated motion in the picking hand. This makes it easier to simply pass over the string when a slide, hammer-on, or pull-off is used, without interrupting the pendulous motion of the picking hand.* This should initially be studied on small sections at a time, until the picking feels comfortable.

The time spent developing this approach to picking should be considered a worthwhile investment, as it will raise your picking control to a level that allows for maximum speed and fluidity, probably otherwise unattainable. Practice patiently, with determination. In addition, it is also very important to practice reading rhythms with ties, dots, rests, eighth notes, sixteenth notes, and triplets, as you can find in books designed to develop sightreading. When reading rhythms, play them on a single open string, and use the same principal of assigning pickstroke direction based on where a note falls within a particular beat. This activity is crucial to developing strict alternate picking.

Continued practice of proper picking technique as applied to the exercises in this book, and to the activity of reading rhythms in sight-reading books will develop a natural, unthinking inclination toward organized picking. Of course, even after developing this most valuable approach to picking, it is sometimes desirable to break the above rules simply because a particular passage works better when picked differently, although such decisions are best made from the vantage point of strength and control by the accomplished player.

Left-Hand Accuracy and Mental Concentration

Many of the examples in this book require a left-hand positioning that facilitates maximum reach and range, such as when a given exercise spans up to seven frets (within one left-hand neck location). This requires that the thumb be positioned low on the neck, and that the left hand be positioned so that it reaches up to the fretboard from below the neck, keeping the fingers parallel to the frets. This is different from the traditional left hand position associated with rock and blues pentatonic soloing, where the left-hand thumb is wrapped around the neck.

In playing a given exercise, pay close attention to notes that tend to be 'glitched'; that is, notes that don't sound fully with a ringing resonance. **You must be mindful and observant to pinpoint those notes that are not sounding fully, and then analyze the cause of the glitch.** This idea cannot be stressed enough. Take the time to observe and analyze the exact cause of the problem, on a given note, within a given exercise. Often the glitched note is caused by not executing the note with adequate velocity on the individual finger that is playing the note.

When working on a given exercise, learn to play it in slow motion, one note at a time. Be mindful not only of playing the notes evenly and continuously, but also of simultaneously keeping your body, hands, and mental attitude RELAXED! Pay close attention to the placement of each note. In this way, playing guitar is very much like the practice of meditation. While you strive to employ your will and intention to control the movements of your fingers, an inner tension naturally arises within your being as you strive to conquer a pattern. When working on new guitar movements, you should periodically remind yourself to relax...to mentally smile from within… to breathe. Avoid having an attitude of striving to impress (yourself and/or others). Playing complex _patterns on the guitar is truly a measure of your ability to concentrate. Concentration translates to your ability to be focused and free from distraction as you play each note._ Distraction arises when you observe what you have just played, and then view it with pleasure or displeasure; or, when you start to think about someone else listening to you perform. This thought process should be released—let go of it. Instead, stay focused on the quality of your execution, on the quality of the sound of the notes.

Look inside a piano, and observe the precision with which each note is sounded. Each hammer, accurately playing each note at the desired moment. Let your fingers be like the hammers inside a piano. Disassociate your striving to play accurately from your emotional review of the results. Even if the notes are not entirely accurate, do not become bogged down in internal feelings of disappointment. And if the notes are performed accurately, do not focus on ideas of self-approval. Always stay focused on the craft, and release internal inclinations of self-approval or disappointment.

As you play an exercise slowly, use the imagery of the mechanical piano hammers. In fact, exaggerate the lifting and independent, abrupt placement of each finger, as if your fingers were like little hammers hitting the strings. _Become aware of the exact cause of any glitched notes, and then solve the problem._ It is a truly simple path, but many guitarists get sidetracked in their mental thought processes before they get around to solving the problem. Have the mentality of being a problem solver. Observe the execution of a difficult passage, playing it slowly with exaggerated left-hand finger placement. Analyze the cause of any glitched notes, and then adjust your hands accordingly. This may seem obvious, but it is actually a level of thinking that is more highly developed among virtuosos, rather than amateurs.

Final Wisdom

When a given study or exercise can be played with some confidence, further adjust your state of mind, to another level. First, relax yourself, physically and mentally. Then simply listen to the notes as you play them, simultaneously singing them internally. **Focus your attention on imagining the sound** of the notes as you play them, rather than on the physical execution. This encourages your hands to be guided by the sound, as opposed to being guided purely by intellectual will. This aspect of musicianship should be intentionally cultivated. Do not underestimate the power of this magical secret.

Finally, be careful not to overstrain the left hand. During intense practice sessions, take timeouts to stretch the arms and hands. If you experience pain from continual and frequent playing, ease up. At that point, you should give your hands a rest for a couple days. To play guitar intensely for a lifetime, one must certainly be sensitive to the periodic pains and micro-injuries that may arise is the hands. These overuse pains (and even swellings) will often disappear if you reduce the intensity and frequency of your guitar playing, and immobilize your wrists and hands (for several days) with wrist braces, available at your local drugstore. Also, playing on a shorter scale length guitar neck (Gibson-style) as opposed to a longer scale length neck (Fender-style) puts a lot less strain on the left hand when working on patterns that require big stretches. That's because the frets are closer together on the short scale length guitar neck. When serious concerns arise with joints and tendons in the hands, do not hesitate in consulting a hand specialist doctor. Take care of your hands, so you can have a lifetime of playing guitar. As a lifetime career guitarist, this author speaks from experience. Now…get busy! (And don't forget to stretch gently.)

Tablature Symbols Key

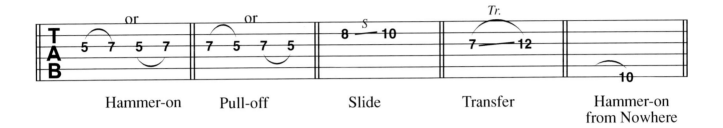

| Hammer-on | Pull-off | Slide | Transfer | Hammer-on from Nowhere |

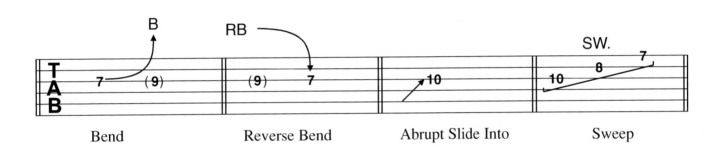

| Bend | Reverse Bend | Abrupt Slide Into | Sweep |